# THE
# ZUNI

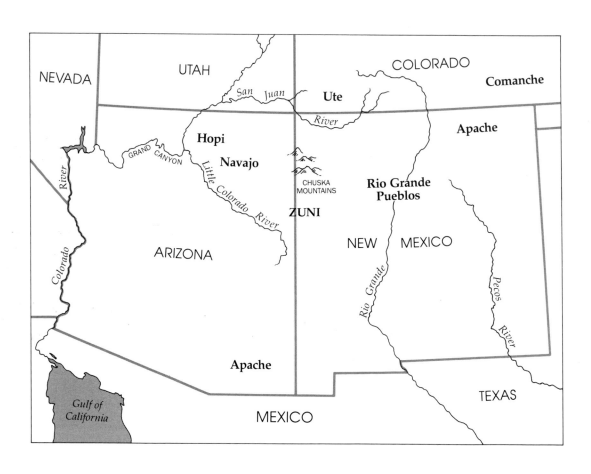

NEVADA

UTAH

COLORADO

Comanche

San Juan

Ute

River

GRAND CANYON

Hopi

Navajo

CHUSKA MOUNTAINS

Apache

Little Colorado River

ZUNI

Rio Grande Pueblos

River

Colorado

ARIZONA

NEW     MEXICO

Rio Grande

Pecos River

Apache

TEXAS

Gulf of California

MEXICO

# THE ZUNI

*Nancy Bonvillain*
*New School for Social Research*

Frank W. Porter III
*General Editor*

CHELSEA HOUSE PUBLISHERS
*New York   Philadelphia*

*On the cover* A collection of contemporary hand-painted Zuni pottery, including a canteen (far right, with strap), two large traditional water jugs, or ollas (right), and three bear figurines (foreground).

**Chelsea House Pubiishers**
*Editorial Director* Richard Rennert
*Executive Managing Editor* Karyn Gullen Browne
*Copy Chief* Robin James
*Picture Editor* Adrian G. Allen
*Creative Director* Robert Mitchell
*Art Director* Joan Ferrigno
*Production Manager* Sallye Scott

**Indians of North America**
*Senior Editor* Sean Dolan
*Native American Specialist* Jack Miller

*Staff for* **THE ZUNI**
*Assistant Editor* Mary B. Sisson
*Assistant Designer* Fran Bonamo
*Picture Researcher* Villette Harris

3  5  7  9  8  6  4  2

Library of Congress Cataloging-in-Publication Data

Bonvillain, Nancy.
    The Zuni / Nancy Bonvillain; Frank W. Porter III, general
editor.
        p.   cm.—(Indians of North America)
    ISBN 0-7910-1689-7.
        0-7910-3478-X (pbk.)
    1. Zuni Indians—History—Juvenile literature. 2. Zuni
Indians—Social life and customs—Juvenile literature.
[1. Zuni Indians. 2. Indians of North America—New Mexico.]
I. Porter, Frank W., 1947–  . II. Title. III. Series: Indians of
North America (Chelsea House Publishers).
E99.Z9866  1995                                    95-1893
973'.04974—dc20                                    CIP
                                                   AC

# CONTENTS

# INDIANS OF NORTH AMERICA

CHELSEA HOUSE PUBLISHERS

# INDIANS OF NORTH AMERICA:
# CONFLICT AND SURVIVAL

## Frank W. Porter III

*The Indians survived our open intention of wiping them out, and since the tide turned they have even weathered our good intentions toward them, which can be much more deadly.*

John Steinbeck
*America and Americans*

When Europeans first reached the North American continent, they found hundreds of tribes occupying a vast and rich country. The newcomers quickly recognized the wealth of natural resources. They were not, however, so quick or willing to recognize the spiritual, cultural, and intellectual riches of the people they called Indians.

*The Indians of North America* examines the problems that develop when people with different cultures come together. For American Indians, the consequences of their interaction with non-Indian people have been both productive and tragic. The Europeans believed they had "discovered" a "New World," but their religious bigotry, cultural bias, and materialistic world view kept them from appreciating and understanding the people who lived in it. All too often they attempted to change the way of life of the indigenous people. The Spanish conquistadores wanted the Indians as a source of labor. The Christian missionaries, many of whom were English, viewed them as potential converts. French traders and trappers used the Indians as a means to obtain pelts. As Francis Parkman, the 19th-century historian, stated, "Spanish civilization crushed the Indian; English civilization scorned and neglected him; French civilization embraced and cherished him."

Nearly 500 years later, many people think of American Indians as curious vestiges of a distant past, waging a futile war to survive in a Space Age society. Even today, our understanding of the history and culture of American Indians is too often derived from unsympathetic, culturally biased, and inaccurate reports. The American Indian, described and portrayed in thousands of movies, television programs, books, articles, and government studies, has either been raised to the status of the "noble savage" or disparaged as the "wild Indian" who resisted the westward expansion of the American frontier.

Where in this popular view are the real Indians, the human beings and communities whose ancestors can be traced back to ice-age hunters? Where are the creative and indomitable people whose sophisticated technologies used the natural resources to ensure their survival, whose military skill might even have prevented European settlement of North America if not for devastating epidemics and disruption of the ecology? Where are the men and women who are today diligently struggling to assert their legal rights and express once again the value of their heritage?

The various Indian tribes of North America, like people everywhere, have a history that includes population expansion, adaptation to a range of regional environments, trade across wide networks, internal strife, and warfare. This was the reality. Europeans justified their conquests, however, by creating a mythical image of the New World and its native people. In this myth, the New World was a virgin land, waiting for the Europeans. The arrival of Christopher Columbus ended a timeless primitiveness for the original inhabitants.

Also part of this myth was the debate over the origins of the American Indians. Fantastic and diverse answers were proposed by the early explorers, missionairies, and settlers. Some thought that the Indians were descended from the Ten Lost Tribes of Israel, others that they were descended from inhabitants of the lost continent of Atlantis. One writer suggested that the Indians had reached North America in another Noah's ark.

A later myth, perpetrated by many historians, focused on the relentless persecution during the past five centuries until only a scattering of these "primitive" people remained to be herded onto reservations. This view fails to chronicle the overt and covert ways in which the Indians successfully coped with the intruders.

All of these myths presented one-sided interpretations that ignored the complexity of European and American events and policies. All left serious questions unanswered. What were the origins of the American Indians? Where did they come from? How and when did they get to the New World? What was their life—their culture—really like?

In the late 1800s, anthropologists and archaeologists in the Smithsonian Institution's newly created Bureau of American Ethnology in Washington,

D.C., began to study scientifically the history and culture of the Indians of North America. They were motivated by an honest belief that the Indians were on the verge of extinction and that along with them would vanish their languages, religious beliefs, technology, myths, and legends. These men and women went out to visit, study, and record data from as many Indian communities as possible before this information was forever lost.

By this time there was a new myth in the national consciousness. American Indians existed as figures in the American past. They had performed a historical mission. They had challenged white settlers who trekked across the continent. Once conquered, however, they were supposed to accept graciously the way of life of their conquerors.

The reality again was different. American Indians resisted both actively and passively. They refused to lose their unique identity, to be assimilated into white society. Many whites viewed the Indians not only as members of a conquered nation but also as "inferior" and "unequal." The rights of the Indians could be expanded, contracted, or modified as the conquerors saw fit. In every generation, white society asked itself what to do with the American Indians. Their answers have resulted in the twists and turns of federal Indian policy.

There were two general approaches. One way was to raise the Indians to a "higher level" by "civilizing" them. Zealous missionaries considered it their Christian duty to elevate the Indian through conversion and scanty education. The other approach was to ignore the Indians until they disappeared under pressure from the ever-expanding white society. The myth of the "vanishing Indian" gave stronger support to the latter option, helping to justify the taking of the Indians' land.

Prior to the end of the 18th century, there was no national policy on Indians simply because the American nation had not yet come into existence. American Indians similarly did not possess a political or social unity with which to confront the various Europeans. They were not homogeneous. Rather, they were loosely formed bands and tribes, speaking nearly 300 languages and thousands of dialects. The collective identity felt by Indians today is a result of their common experiences of defeat and/or mistreatment at the hands of whites.

During the colonial period, the British crown did not have a coordinated policy toward the Indians of North America. Specific tribes (most notably the Iroquois and the Cherokee) became military and political pawns used by both the crown and the individual colonies. The success of the American Revolution brought no immediate change. When the United States acquired new territory from France and Mexico in the early 19th century, the federal government wanted to open this land to settlement by homesteaders. But the Indian tribes that lived on this land had signed treaties with European governments assuring their title to the land. Now the United States assumed legal responsibility for honoring these treaties.

At first, President Thomas Jefferson believed that the Louisiana Purchase contained sufficient land for both the Indians and the white population. Within a generation, though, it became clear that the Indians would not be allowed to remain. In the 1830s the federal government began to coerce the eastern tribes to sign treaties agreeing to relinquish their ancestral land and move west of the Mississippi River. Whenever these negotiations failed, President Andrew Jackson used the military to remove the Indians. The southeastern tribes, promised food and transportation during their removal to the West, were instead forced to walk the "Trail of Tears." More than 4,000 men, woman, and children died during this forced march. The "removal policy" was successful in opening the land to homesteaders, but it created enormous hardships for the Indians.

By 1871 most of the tribes in the United States had signed treaties ceding most or all of their ancestral land in exchange for reservations and welfare. The treaty terms were intended to bind both parties for all time. But in the General Allotment Act of 1887, the federal government changed its policy again. Now the goal was to make tribal members into individual landowners and farmers, encouraging their absorption into white society. This policy was advantageous to whites who were eager to acquire Indian land, but it proved disastrous for the Indians. One hundred thirty-eight million acres of reservation land were subdivided into tracts of 160, 80, or as little as 40 acres, and allotted tribe members on an individual basis. Land owned in this way was said to have "trust status" and could not be sold. But the surplus land—all Indian land not allotted to individuals—was opened (for sale) to white settlers. Ultimately, more than 90 million acres of land were taken from the Indians by legal and illegal means.

The resulting loss of land was a catastrophe for the Indians. It was necessary to make it illegal for Indians to sell their land to non-Indians. The Indian Reorganization Act of 1934 officially ended the allotment period. Tribes that voted to accept the provisions of this act were reorganized, and an effort was made to purchase land within preexisting reservations to restore an adequate land base.

Ten years later, in 1944, federal Indian policy again shifted. Now the federal government wanted to get out of the "Indian business." In 1953 an act of Congress named specific tribes whose trust status was to be ended "at the earliest possible time." This new law enabled the United States to end unilaterally, whether the Indians wished it or not, the special status that protected the land in Indian tribal reservations. In the 1950s federal Indian policy was to transfer federal responsibility and jurisdiction to state governments, encourage the physical relocation of Indian peoples from reservations to urban areas, and hasten the termination, or extinction, of tribes.

Between 1954 and 1962 Congress passed specific laws authorizing the termination of more than 100 tribal groups. The stated purpose of the termination policy was to ensure the full and complete integration of Indians into American society. However, there is a less benign way to interpret this legislation. Even as termination was being discussed in Congress, 133 separate bills were introduced to permit the transfer of trust land ownership from Indians to non-Indians.

With the Johnson administration in the 1960s the federal government began to reject termination. In the 1970s yet another Indian policy emerged. Known as "self-determination," it favored keeping the protective role of the federal government while increasing tribal participation in, and control of, important areas of local government. In 1983 President Reagan, in a policy statement on Indian affairs, restated the unique "government is government" relationship of the United States with the Indians. However, federal programs since then have moved toward transferring Indian affairs to individual states, which have long desired to gain control of Indian land and resources.

As long as American Indians retain power, land, and resources that are coveted by the states and the federal government, there will continue to be a "clash of cultures," and the issues will be contested in the courts, Congress, the White House, and even in the international human rights community. To give all Americans a greater comprehension of the issues and conflicts involving American Indians today is a major goal of this series. These issues are not easily understood, nor can these conflicts be readily resolved. The study of North American Indian history and culture is a necessary and important step toward that comprehension. All Americans must learn the history of the relations between the Indians and the federal government, recognize the unique legal status of the Indians, and understand the heritage and cultures of the Indians of North America.

*Ancient corn grinders or metates lay in an Anasazi ruin located in Arizona. The Zunis'*
*ancestors first came to the American Southwest approximately 10,000 years ago.*

# 1

# THE
# MIDDLE
# PLACE

In the beginning, say the Zunis, the only being who lived was Awonawilona, a deity both male and female. Nothing else existed, except some fog and steam. Then Awonawilona created the clouds and waters from its breath, and the rest of the universe was formed.

The universe created by Awonawilona consists of nine layers. The earth, a large circular island surrounded by oceans, occupies the middle level. The lakes, rivers, and springs on the earth are connected to the oceans by underground linkages. The sky layer is an upsidedown bowl of stone, resting above the earth. The other eight layers of the universe are each home to different kinds of animals, birds, and trees.

At first people lived under the earth's surface in the fourth and innermost layer of the universe, deep inside the body of Earth Mother. The people did not look like humans today. Instead their bodies were covered with slime, they had webbed hands and feet, and they had tails. They had no idea how strange they looked because it was dark where they lived and they could not see well. Then the Sun Father decided to bring the people out to the surface of the earth because he was lonely and had no one to give him offerings and prayers. Sun Father told his twin sons, the War Gods, to lead the Zunis out from inside the earth. The War Gods helped the people climb up a ladder to the surface of the earth and, once they were there, changed their appearance. The slime on the people's bodies disappeared and their hands and feet became normal. Deities and priests instructed the people to recite prayers, make offerings, and conduct ceremonies to honor Sun Father and other spirit powers. In return, the spirits gave people blessings and protection.

The Zunis remained near their place of emergence for a time. Then deities told the Zunis to go forth and find the middle place, or *itiwana*, of the world, where they should build their villages. Important holy men called Rain Priests led the people on a journey that took many years. Each time they chose a place to settle, some misfortune occurred that forced them to move again. These misfortunes were signs from the spirits that the people had not yet found the itiwana of the world.

At last the Zunis met an old man who was a powerful Rain Priest. When the Zunis' own Rain Priest prayed with the old man, a heavy rainstorm fell. Suddenly a water spider came by, spread out its six legs, and told the people that the itiwana was directly under its heart. The Zuni knew its message to be true and set about building their villages. They built one village at the itiwana and six others at locations marked off by the six legs of the water spider.

The Zuni then erected an altar at the exact site of the itiwana. On the altar they placed sacred objects belonging to the Rain Priests as reminders of the people's journey and of their duty to honor the powerful deities who led them there. The altar remains today at the center of the village of Zuni. On it rests a stone that contains the eternal beating heart of the itiwana of the world.

The Zunis' story of their creation, emergence, and discovery of the itiwana situates them literally in the center of the world. Not surprisingly, they feel a strong spiritual and emotional connection to their locale. They and their ancestors lived for centuries in lands along the banks of the Zuni River in western New Mexico. Their beautiful homeland contains a diversity of terrain and resources, including flat plains, plateaus, deserts, woodlands, foothills, and mountains. On the plains and desert grasslands grow shrubs, herbs, cactus, rabbitbrush, and yucca. Oak, spruce, juniper, and piñon trees are abundant in woodlands and mountainous regions. The mountains and foothills are inhabited by many animals such as elk, deer, antelope, mountain sheep, bears, and foxes. Rabbits, mice, squirrels, and reptiles abound in all areas.

Today the Zunis reside in one large town, called Zuni, and several small suburbs located along nearby rivers and streams. Before the arrival of Europeans in the early 16th century, the Zunis lived in six villages, all situated within a 25-mile area and with access to good farmland. Zuni territory extended well beyond the area occupied by the villages, to the Zuni Mountains in the east and north and the lower, more desertlike area to the west and south.

The Zunis made good use of the resources available in their territory, and their land has supported people from the time of the earliest arrival of their ancestors in the Southwest approximately 10,000 years ago. These early inhabitants created a civilization known to archaeologists as the Desert Tradition. Desert Tradition sites have been discovered at Concho in present-day eastern Arizona and at Bat Cave and Tularosa Cave in northern and central New Mexico. During the Desert period, people did not have permanent settlements. They shifted their camps from time to time, adjusting their settlements to changes in plant growth and animal populations. Due to the scarcity of permanent sources

*Buffalo (such as the one pictured above) formed an important part of the food supply of all the peoples of the American Southwest.*

of food, Desert camps were small, consisting of no more than a few families. The Desert peoples hunted animals, including several species of now-extinct horses, elephants, and great bison, for meat to use as food and for hides to use for clothing and shelter. They also gathered wild plants to eat and invented specialized technologies for preparing and cooking plant foods. One such technology that has survived to modern times is the use of *metates*, specialized grinding stones for making meal of different kinds of seeds and nuts.

Thousands of years after Desert peoples first entered the American Southwest, their descendants learned how to grow some of their own food. The earliest evidence of farming in the region dates from approximately 5,000 years ago. The Desert peoples apparently borrowed farming methods from other tribes living farther south in present-day Mexico. These techniques gradually

*Earthen pots were first made in the American Southwest over 1,000 years ago by the Mogollon peoples. This pot, made in the Anasazi tradition, is approximately 800 years old.*

spread into the present-day American Southwest through a process called cultural diffusion, the borrowing of skills by one group of people from neighboring groups.

The first plant grown by Native American farmers was corn—in fact, for approximately 2,000 years corn was the only crop cultivated in America. Then, about 3,000 years ago, Native American farmers began to cultivate varieties of beans and squash. These three plants—corn, beans, and squash—have remained staples of southwestern cuisine, including that of the modern Zuni.

Although Desert peoples farmed, they combined farming with their earlier way of life, continuing to hunt animals, gather wild plants, and live in small nomadic groups. Then, in about 300 B.C., for reasons that remain unknown, a profound cultural change took place in the societies of the American Southwest. A new culture developed called the Mogollon Tradition. Mogollon peoples added many innovations to the older Desert

Tradition, changing their settlements, economies, and technology.

The most obvious contrast between the Mogollon and Desert cultures is that Mogollon peoples lived in permanent villages. They built small settlements of approximately 100 people, living in rectangular or circular houses made of clay and stone. Ruins of Mogollon villages have been found at Forestdale and Black River in Arizona and at Cibola and Mimbres in New Mexico.

Farming and agricultural products became more central to the lives and economies of the Mogollon peoples. Corn was prepared by first drying and crushing the kernels and then grinding them into meal using a grinding stone. The resulting cornmeal was moistened with water and cooked on heated stones. Fresh corn was also simply roasted over coals. Mogollon peoples dried beans to preserve them for later use; when they wanted to prepare the dried beans for meals, they soaked them and boiled them in water. Squash was either boiled in water when fresh or dried for later use. The seeds of squash, which are higher in calories, vitamins, and calcium than the flesh, were dried and stored for winter meals. In addition to the staples of corn, beans, and squash, the Mogollon peoples raised tobacco as well as cotton and sunflowers, which were cultivated for their vitamin- and calorie-rich seeds.

The Mogollon peoples expanded their inventory of tools and utensils. They made dishes, hammers, axes, hoes, bows, arrows, and a variety of grinding utensils such as metates, mortars, and pestles from stone, wood, bone, and shell. Mogollon artists used tools to carve masks and effigies from stone and wood, while weavers used cotton (also introduced into the area by Mexican Indians) to make both plain and fancy cloth. In addition to these innovations, the Mogollon peoples began making earthen pottery, forming pots, bowls, and jars of different sizes and shapes to use for cooking and for carrying and storing foods and supplies.

By about A.D. 700 or 800 the Zunis' Mogollon ancestors had established permanent settlements in present-day Zuni territory. One such settlement is a village called White Mound, which contains groups of pit houses made of sandstone blocks and slabs and dug several feet into the ground to protect residents against outside cold and heat. In each house a series of rooms 10 to 12 feet across is arranged in a line. A single nuclear family probably lived in each room, and a house probably contained a group of related families. In addition to the pit houses, storerooms were built at ground level to hold equipment and dried foods. Farmland was located outside the clusters of houses and storerooms.

Other Mogollon villages in present-day Zuni territory include Kiatuthlanna, built in A.D. 800 or 900. Kiatuthlanna was larger than White Mound; its 18 homes held an estimated population of 75 to 100 people. In a later village named Allantown, built around A.D. 1000, houses constructed at ground level had begun to replace pit houses as the typical form of residence. Allantown and other Mogollon villages also contained *kivas* (pronounced KEY-vas), special buildings where religious ceremonies were held.

Many innovative pottery designs, especially painted motifs, have been unearthed in Mogollon village digs. The artists initially used white paste and mineral paints to make black-on-white designs but eventually developed the use of glaze in the colors of green and cinnamon. The designs themselves also changed, from thin lines to wider and more blocky designs that included geometric shapes and naturalistic figures.

Another new culture developed in the American Southwest around A.D. 1100. Called the Anasazi Tradition, it covered a large area, including present-day New Mexico, most of Arizona, and the southern portions of Utah and Colorado. The largest Anasazi villages were concentrated in the region known today as Four Corners, where the states of Arizona, New Mexico, Utah, and Colorado meet. Well-known ruins of Anasazi settlements include those of Canyon de Chelly and Kayenta in Arizona, Mesa Verde in Colorado, and Chaco Canyon in New Mexico. While the Zunis' ancestors were on the periphery of Anasazi territory, they had contact with and were influenced by a number of Anasazi settlements, especially the one at Chaco Canyon.

Early in the Anasazi period, around A.D. 1100 or 1200, a Zuni settlement called the Village of the Great Kivas was built. The village contained three large masonry structures, varying in size from 6 to 60 rooms, all built at ground level, as well as nine round ceremonial kivas, seven of which were about the size of a single house. The remaining two kivas were much larger, measuring 51 and 78 feet in diameter, and were built in front of the village. These great kivas have benches attached to their interior walls, presumably used for seating during rituals, and also contain two vaults beneath the main floor.

During the Anasazi period the Zunis' ancestors built several villages in valleys along the Zuni River and its tributaries. Some of these settlements were situated near cliffs that gave residents protection from wind and snowstorms. By the 13th century the Zunis' ancestors began to construct villages on top of mesas, giving the inhabitants a clear view of all approaches to the village and making defense of the village easier. One such village is Atsinna, located on a mesa known as Inscription Rock. The entire village of Atsinna formed a rectangle, measuring 215 by 300 feet; its approximately 1,000 rooms were joined together in housing clusters. Some of the houses had only ground-floor rooms, while others had rooms on a second and third floor as well. The houses at Atsinna all faced inward, opening onto a large inner plaza.

Sometime in the 14th century Anasazi people in the Four Corners region suddenly abandoned their large towns and settled in smaller villages. The reason for this move is not certain, but most modern researchers suggest that a dras-

*The Anasazi peoples built a number of impressive cities, the ruins of which can still be seen today. The photograph above shows the Anasazi ruins at Pueblo Bonito, in Chaco Canyon, New Mexico.*

*The ruins of the Zuni village of Hawikuh emerge from a dig. The first of the six Zuni villages visited by the Spanish conquistadores, Hawikuh was probably established around the 14th century.*

tic climatic change, most probably a series of lengthy droughts, impelled the move. Some of the Anasazi people then established villages along the Rio Grande in New Mexico, using water from the large river to irrigate their farms. Other people, including the Zunis and the nearby Hopis, remained away from the Rio Grande in the dry desert lands of New Mexico and Arizona.

Although the Zunis did not move to the Rio Grande, during this period many people did move from towns located in the eastern half of Zuni territory into towns located farther west. The six Zuni villages discovered by the Spanish conquistadores in the 16th century—Halona ("red ant place" and the home of the itiwana), Hawikuh, Kiakima ("house of eagles"), Matsaki, Kwakina ("town of the entrance place"), and Kechipauan ("gypsum place")—were established as a result of this migration.

Local and regional trade was an important feature of life in the American Southwest. The Zunis traded directly with their neighbors and, through trade networks, with Native Americans living in other areas. As early as A.D. 600–900 the Zunis' ancestors had trade relations with peoples in Mexico, California, and the Great Plains. By A.D. 1250 Zuni villages, especially Hawikuh, had become centers for intertribal trade and were visited by peoples from throughout the American Southwest and adjacent regions. The Zunis traded corn, salt taken from Zuni Salt Lake (located approximately 60 miles south of Halona), turquoise from local mines,

and buffalo hides obtained by Zuni hunters on expeditions into the Great Plains, as well as cotton cloth, jewelry, baskets, pottery, moccasins, and a distinctive blue paint. In return the Zunis received pottery, copper, and parrot feathers from Mexico; buffalo hides from the Great Plains; and seashells and coral from California.

The Zunis maintained peaceful relations with most of their neighbors in the Southwest. Many of these peoples, including the Hopis, Tewas, Tanos, and Keres, were culturally similar to the Zuni; consequently, these groups are often grouped together as the Pueblo Indians. Although Pueblo Indians share many cultural features, they are distinct peoples and speak different languages—indeed, the Pueblo languages come from several entirely separate linguistic families, and Zuni is different from all other languages spoken in the region. Linguists today are uncertain as to whether Zuni is a language isolate, with no known connections to any other language, or whether it belongs to a language family called Penutian, in which case it is a remote relative of languages spoken in parts of California. The language of the nearby Hopi belongs to a family called Uto-Aztecan, distantly related to the language spoken by Aztecs in Mexico. The Pueblo Indians who live along the Rio Grande speak languages belonging to two other language families, Tanoan and Keresan. One result of the different languages used among the Pueblo Indians is that the Zunis are not called by the name they call themselves,

*The village of the Acoma Pueblos, photographed in 1904. The word Zuni is the Acoman name for the tribe that calls itself the A-shiwi.*

the A-shiwi (pronounced with a long *a*). *Zuni* comes from a word in a Keresan language used by the Acoma Pueblos to refer to the A-shiwis; it was picked up by the Spanish from the Acomas and has since come into general use.

By the time the Spanish arrived to misname them, the Zunis had long established a stable, peaceful, and prosperous way of life in the itiwana of the world. Not only had they managed to develop the material resources of their relatively harsh surroundings, but they had also created a complex society intimately linked with their natural environment. ▲

*A Zuni woman carries her baby over the threshold of her home. The Zunis have numerous ceremonies to mark important events in people's lives, including birth, adolescence, and death.*

# THE ZUNI AND THE RAW PEOPLE

For the people of the itiwana, religion was the center of life, giving meaning to all activities. Success in farming, childbirth, and many other aspects of life was considered to be due to the aid of the Raw People, the Zuni name for the many powerful deities and spirits in Zuni religion. These spirits were called Raw People because they ate raw foods as well as the cooked foods given to them as offerings by humans, who were called the Cooked People or Daylight People. In addition to making offerings, humans expressed respect and gratitude to the Raw People by saying prayers and performing rituals in their honor. In exchange, Raw People protected humans and gave them long lives, healthy children, personal courage, bountiful crops, successful hunts, and good fortune.

The many kinds of Raw People were associated with various natural forces or entities. Some Raw People were believed to be the spirits of animals, birds, or objects such as the sun, earth, and celestial bodies. Three very powerful Raw People were Earth Mother, Sun Father, and Moonlight-Giving Mother. Earth Mother was the place of life's origin, while Sun Father and Moonlight-Giving Mother gave humans light and good fortune (they were also husband and wife). Sun Father was considered especially important because he was the source of daylight, which was considered tantamount to life by the Zunis; indeed, the word for "daylight" and the word for "life" are the same in the Zuni language. Because of Sun Father's special role, sunrise was considered the most sacred time of day.

Other Raw People were associated with directions or with specific locations, such as lakes and mountains. According to Zuni cosmology, the world is oriented to six sacred directions: north, east, south, west, above (the zenith), and below (the nadir). In addition to these directions, there is the iti-wana, or middle, that connects the various elements of the universe. Directions in space help to set the boundaries of the world and to orient individuals to their places in it. Each direction is associated with certain colors, animals, birds, and trees. For the Zunis, this sys-tem of linkages underscored the spiri-tual unity and interconnection of all life in the universe.

The various elements of the world were kept alive and in balance by the efforts of the Raw People. In return for their protection and benevolence, the Zunis gave the Raw People food such as cornmeal (sometimes mixed with crushed turquoise, shell, or coral), tobacco smoke, and small portions of cooked food. They also offered the dei-ties sacred ceremonial sticks, called prayer sticks, that the men would make from the wood of willow trees by carv-

*Zuni ceremonial masks, used to represent certain Raw People known as kachinas.*

ing faces into a piece of wood and decorating it with paint and feathers. Although only men could make the sticks, both women and men offered them to spirits or ancestors. The offering of prayer sticks formed an important part of many ceremonies, especially those marking the summer and winter solstices (June 21st and December 21st).

In addition to honoring the Raw People, Zuni rituals were used to mark various critical stages in people's lives, including birth, puberty, marriage, and death. When a baby was born, its female relatives performed a variety of important duties. The baby's maternal grandmother would assist her daughter in the birth, but once the baby was born its paternal grandmother would come to the home and recite prayers asking the Raw People to protect the baby. She then would bathe the baby, rub ashes on its body, prepare a bed of warm sand for it to lie in, and remain with mother and child for eight days. At sunrise on the eighth day after birth, the paternal grandmother would wash the baby's head, place cornmeal in its hands, and then take the baby out into the dawn air, facing east toward the rising sun. While other female relatives sprinkled cornmeal toward the east, the grandmother would offer a prayer of blessing:

Now this is the day.
Our child,
Into the daylight
You will go standing.
Now this day
Our sun father,

Having come out standing to his
sacred place,
Our child,
It is your day.
The flesh of the white corn,
Prayer meal,
To our sun father
This prayer meal we offer.
May your road be fulfilled
Reaching to the road of your sun
father.

This prayer reflected a number of Zuni beliefs. The Zunis thought of life as a road that every individual follows according to his or her own destiny. Sun Father assigned a specific road to each newborn baby, and all people hoped to live until they reached the proper end of their roads. Accidents or evil beings could interfere, however, and cause a premature death. Consequently a newborn's grandmother prayed that her grandchild would be protected and allowed to live out his or her appointed road. The paternal grandmother also chose the baby's name, but babies were not named immediately after birth. Instead, the family would wait until they were sure that the infant was a healthy one and was likely to survive. Usually the name given the baby was the same as that of a relative on either side of the family who had lived a long life.

When a young Zuni girl reached puberty, another important set of rituals would take place. The adolescent girl would go to the home of her paternal grandmother, where she would spend a full day grinding corn—an act significant on both a secular and religious level. Grinding corn into meal was one of the primary duties of Zuni women, so in completing this ritual the girl would perform the practical work expected of adult women. But corn was also considered a sacred plant by the Zunis, a gift brought to them by six Raw People known as the Corn Maidens. Corn was believed to be the literal flesh of these powerful Raw People and to have great spiritual power; consequently, it was used in practically every religious ceremony—and only women could keep, prepare, and distribute this essential substance. The performance of the corn-grinding cermony thus indicated that a girl was now old enough to take on the important religious responsibilities of adult Zuni women, as well as their secular duties.

After a young lady hit puberty, she was expected to become a wife. After a man and woman decided that they wanted to marry, the woman would consult with her mother to make sure that the union met with the family's approval. Then for several weeks the couple would attempt a trial marriage. The man would come to the woman's home at night, stay with her, and leave before dawn. During this time either the man or the woman could choose not to marry. If the woman decided against marriage, the matter ended immediately, but if the man changed his mind, he had to give the woman a gift before the bond was broken.

In most cases the couple would continue their relationship and become offi-

cially married. The Zuni marriage ceremony was fairly simple, and was both performed and celebrated by various exchanges of gifts. Female relatives of the woman and man involved would give each other presents of food, clothing, and jewelry. As part of this ceremonial exchange of gifts, the woman would grind a large supply of corn to present to her mother-in-law. The mother-in-law would accept the cornmeal and give the bride a set of festive clothing. The couple would then return to the bride's home. The next morning the husband would leave after sunrise and return in the early evening to share dinner with his new family. At this point the couple would be considered husband and wife by the community.

The marriage ceremony could be further streamlined if a man decided to propose marriage without prior consultation or discussion. In this case the man would simply bring a number of gifts to the woman's house and place them in the center of the room. The woman's father would then ask him to explain his intentions. The man would state his desire for marriage, and the father would respond by saying, "It is up to my daughter." At that point, the woman could accept or reject the proposal.

Death among the Zunis marked a time of sorrow and solemn ritual, in contrast to the informality of marriage rites. The deceased person's paternal aunt would come to the home and bathe the body in suds made from a yucca plant. She would then rub cornmeal on the

*A young Zuni woman grinds corn in a metate. Cornmeal was used both as a food staple and as a sacred substance in religious rituals.*

*A kiva photographed in an Anasazi ruin located at Aztec, New Mexico. Unlike this kiva (and those of many other Pueblo tribes), the kivas of the Zunis are square.*

body and dress it in new clothes, making a gash in each garment so that spirits of the clothes could accompany the person's soul on its journey to the afterworld. Relatives would come to the deceased's home and express their grief through words and tears, and the deceased's brothers would dig a grave and carry the body out for burial. The body was placed in the grave so that the head faced east, the direction of the rising sun. A number of the deceased's possessions were placed in the grave for the soul's use in the afterworld, while the rest of the deceased's personal belongings were later burned or buried in a separate spot.

After the burial a four-day period of intense mourning was observed by the surviving spouse. The spouse had to stay away from fire, bathe only in cold water, avoid meat and salt, remain quiet, and keep away from others as much as possible. Most Zuni couples resided with the wife's relatives; consequently, if a wife died, the surviving husband had to leave the house and return permanently to his mother's or sister's home—a practice reflected in a Zuni saying, "Death takes two, not one." The saying also reflected the belief that during the four days of mourning the deceased's soul might try to take a companion such as a close family member along on the journey to the afterworld. During this period the soul stayed in the village and sometimes made itself known to the living by scratching on surfaces, opening and closing doors, or appearing in dreams.

At the end of the four days the soul would leave the village of the living and travel west to the village where souls reside. This village was located at the bottom of a sacred lake, two days' journey from the town of Zuni. If death was premature, however, the soul could not reach its final destination immediately but had to wait at a spot called Spirit Place, located one mile west of Zuni, until the time it should have reached the end of the road given to it at birth by Sun Father. When its appointed end finally came, the waiting soul could join its companions in the village under the lake.

The Zunis believed that the living and dead were eternally linked. The living had to honor the spirits of deceased ancestors, family members, and even enemy soldiers with prayers, food, and rituals performed for their pleasure. In return, the spirits would protect the living from harm and, if properly honored, would even transform themselves into rain clouds and bless the living with valuable rainfall.

The living and the dead were connected in yet another way, through the kachina impersonators. According to Zuni myth, during the tribe's wandering before finding the itiwana some children were killed beside a lake. The itiwana was found, but the parents of the children missed them terribly and were always sad. To cheer them up, the spirits of the children (who had formed the village of souls underneath the lake) came to visit, bringing blessings and rainfall. These were the first kachinas (*kokko* in

Zuni). Although their visits brought the Zunis much joy, every time the kachinas returned to the village of the dead, they took the soul of a living person with them. The Zunis finally discussed this problem with the kachinas, who decided that they would no longer visit the Zunis in person but would only visit as rainfall. So that they might still enjoy dancing for the living, they allowed the Zunis to impersonate them by dressing in their costumes and masks and mimicking their dances and behavior.

Impersonating a kachina was no ordinary task. Kachinas had great magical power and in a sense possessed their impersonators. The masks and costumes used by kachina impersonators were made and handled with a great deal of care and religious ceremony; they were considered both sacred and alive and perfectly capable of harming or killing a disrespectful or sinful impersonator. In addition, kachina impersonators had to perform intricate and lengthy public dances to properly honor the kachinas; these dances required days of rehearsal and sometimes lasted for hours. Creative Zunis could discover new kachinas to impersonate or invent new dances to perform provided that they were considered appropriate by religious leaders, but the older forms were always considered both more powerful and holier.

In order to maintain the kachina tradition, six specialized ritual groups called kachina societies emerged among the Zunis. All Zuni men were members of one of the six Zuni kachina societies, which performed dances four times

every year—just before the winter solstice, later in winter, in summer, and at harvesttime. On these days the dancers would don their masks and costumes and enter the village at dawn. Led by their kachina chief and watched by almost everyone in the village, the dancers would perform in the town's public plazas. While kachina dances obviously had great religious significance, they were also loved because of their beauty. Indeed, one of the expressed purposes of the kachina dances was to provide entertainment for the village, and audience members could request that a particularly good dance be repeated again and again.

Kachina societies also held ceremonies in kivas. Each of the six kivas in Zuni was associated with a specific kachina society. Zuni kivas were special square-shaped rooms that were entered and exited by a ladder that extended through an opening in the ceiling; inside were large open spaces where dances and rituals were performed, with benches built against the walls to provide seating. In addition, kivas contained smaller rooms where highly secret rituals were conducted.

Zuni boys were inducted into kachina societies by their ceremonial fathers, a kind of godfather chosen by the boy's parents. A ceremonial father would induct his godson into his own kachina society when the boy was about five or six years old. During this initiation ceremony, the boy was washed by the wife of his ceremonial father, then carried by the ceremonial father to his kiva. Several boys were inducted at once, and when they all arrived at the kiva, adult members of the kachina society would enter dressed as kachinas and whip the boys to purify them. Although the whipping itself was usually quite gentle and painless, the experience was nonetheless an intimidating one for the boys because at this point they usually did not know that the kachinas were human impersonators. When the whipping ended, the ceremonial fathers would take the purified children home.

When the purified boys reached about 10 or 12 years of age, the second stage of initiation into the kachina societies occurred. The boys were again taken by their ceremonial fathers to the kivas and were whipped (usually more severely than during the initial purification) by the kachinas. This time, when the whipping ended, the impersonators would remove their masks, revealing to the boys that they were indeed human beings. The two groups then reversed roles, with the boys putting on the masks and whipping the adults. In this way, the boys gained the knowledge necessary for them to carry on the kachina society rituals.

*Shalako impersonators participate in a religious ritual in this 1896 photograph. The annual Shalako ceremony is still performed and is one of the few contemporary Zuni ceremonies that is open to observation by non-Zunis.*

The kachina societies were only six of the many Zuni religious societies. Each year, 12 Zuni men were chosen to impersonate six deities known as the *Shalakos*. The Shalakos were powerful, birdlike beings who performed dances in new homes built especially for them every year in the late fall and brought good fortune, abundant crops, and many children. Shalako impersonators wore especially distinctive masks and costumes that made them over 10 feet tall.

Another special group of masked gods was made up of 10 ritual clowns called the Mudheads or *Koyemshi*. Unlike the Shalako, the Koyemshi appeared in numerous dances and public rituals throughout the year, and different people could imitate a particular Koyemshi at different events. According to Zuni myth, the Koyemshi were the result of a sexual liaison between a brother and sister and, because of this incest, were both idiotic and impotent. Koyemshi impersonators wore mud-colored masks with foolish-looking faces and a short kilt of black cloth. Instead of wearing underclothes, Koyemshi impersonators had their penises tied down with cotton cord to symbolize both the childishness and the infertility of the Koyemshi. Each Koyemshi had a distinct personality; for example, one Koyemshi was a terrific coward, one was incredibly afraid of shadows and dark things, and one mistakenly believed that he was invisible. Koyemshi impersonators engaged in comical, outrageous, and often obscene behavior, exposing themselves, shouting obscenities, and making fun of spectators, kachina dancers, and priests.

Despite their foolish and unacceptable behavior (which also served as an example of how not to act), the Koyemshi were revered by the Zunis. They were believed to be Raw People of great antiquity, predating even the kachinas, and consequently were considered to have great power to bring fortune and rain. The Koyemshi's great power also made them potentially dangerous. At a certain point in the year the Zunis were expected to give gifts to the Koyemshi impersonators. To begrudge the Koyemshi anything at this time, even in thought, was considered an invitation to disaster.

Another type of ritual clown was the *Neweekwe*. While they often appeared at the same events as the Koyemshi, the Neweekwe were not impersonators of Raw People but were instead members of perhaps the most remarkable of the many Zuni medicine societies. All of these societies performed dances and rituals intended to cure illness, but the Neweekwe were the only such society to engage in ritual clowning. Like the Koyemshi impersonators, members of the Neweekwe Medicine Society often behaved in a wild or obscene manner, but unlike the Koyemshi, they were not expected to take on specific personas. Consequently, the Neweekwe often engaged in far more sophisticated forms of clowning than the childish Koyemshi, including sometimes-biting parodies of current events. Since the Neweekwe Medicine Society specialized in curing stomach ailments, Neweekwe clowns would demonstrate the strength of their stomachs by drinking undrinkable fluids, such as urine, and eating inedible things, such as ashes, pebbles, wood chips, and feces.

While most Zuni medicine societies did not go to the extremes of the Neweekwe in demonstrating their effectiveness, members of some medicine societies did engage in especially dramatic displays of their skills. Healers belonging to the Snake Medicine Society and the Little Fire Society bathed in fire, swallowed fire, and danced on hot coals without getting burned. Members of the Sword People bathed in icy water in the wintertime and swallowed swords and sticks without getting cut. These spectacular public rituals not only displayed the powers of the various medicine societies but were also believed to bring good health to the community in general. Both men and women could learn to perform these rituals by volunteering to join a medicine society. In addition to learning a society's signature dramatic exploit, members of a medicine society learned the healing properties of roots, plants, massages, and rituals. Although some medicine societies relied more on medical cures and others more on ritual ones, every medicine society had its specialty and would treat patients whenever their services were needed—although a patient who had received successful medical treatment from a society was often compelled to join that society.

The Zuni, like all peoples throughout the world, had a complex theory of causes and treatments of disease. Most ailments were believed to have a spiritual or supernatural cause; consequently, it was believed necessary to accurately diagnose the spiritual cause and treat it through religious ritual rather than simply eliminating obvious symptoms. Although there were many potential reasons for illness, most ailments were believed to result from the actions of spirits or witches. Spirits could harm someone who had violated ritual rules or had not properly honored deities and ancestors. Witches—spiteful, jealous, and malicious humans with magical knowledge—would cause harm in retaliation for a slight or out of envy for another's good fortune.

Spirits and witches often caused illness by magically shooting a foreign object such as a pebble, a piece of wood, or a feather into their victims. The harmful object had to be found and extracted for the patient to recover. Certain healers were able to see into a patient's body, locate the hidden object, and draw it to the surface either with an eagle feather or by sucking on the body. These healers gained their knowledge from the spirit of the bear, the most powerful of animal patrons.

Witches could also cause illness by reciting harmful spells over objects that used to belong to the intended victim, such as nail clippings, bits of hair, or pieces of clothing. Such spells could cause the victim to sicken or die. In this situation, a healer would attempt to break the spell through prayers and rituals. If the healer or patient knew the

*Koyemshi impersonators gather in a public square. Although the Koyemshi behaved in childish and sometimes obscene ways, they were considered powerful and sacred beings.*

identity of the witch, the patient's family could try to convince or force the witch into confessing and removing the spell.

Yet another important group of religious societies consisted of priesthoods. The most powerful was the Rain Priesthood—not surprisingly, given the importance of rain to the Zunis' survival. The Rain Priests were all men of high moral character; they avoided spiritually polluting arguments and conflicts and derived their knowledge and powers from the Rain-Bringing Spirits, who were among the most honored of deities.

One of the primary duties of the Rain Priests was to go on retreats to pray and perform rituals that would bring rain to the Zunis. Some of the rituals involved sacred bundles, which contained holy objects of great power such as corn, cornmeal, seeds, feathers, prayer sticks, and stone effigies of spirit animals. The Rain Priesthood was made up of small groups of priests who would conduct four- or eight-day retreats in succession throughout the year, so that the community would never be without their spiritual aid.

Another prestigious group was the Bow Priesthood, which was believed to have obtained its power from the twin War Gods who led the Zuni out of the earth in ancient times. Membership in the Bow Priesthood was required for warriors who had killed an enemy in combat; by joining the priesthood, the warrior obtained protection against the spirit of his deceased enemy, who would otherwise seek revenge. The responsibil-

ities of the Bow Priesthood were both more secular and more martial than those of the Rain Priesthood. Bow Priests were responsible for carrying out warfare and keeping order in the villages; guarding the many trails that the Zuni used to conduct local, regional, and long-distance trade; and carrying out the decisions made by the Zunis' ruling council of religious leaders, which consisted of the heads of various religious orders, including the Rain Priesthoods, kachina societies, and medicine societies. Bow Priests also conducted the trials of people accused of witchcraft and performed the execution of unrepentant witches. (It should be noted that, in Zuni society, the crime of witchcraft legally encompassed not only the casting of evil spells but also a variety of less magical criminal acts, including murder.)

The common religious beliefs and practices of the Zunis helped keep their community strong and united. Private and public ceremonies were a focus of people's activity all year long, and anyone who was not planning, rehearsing, or conducting religious rituals at any given time participated as an audience member. Zuni religious societies also decreased factionalism within the community by splitting their members' allegiances between their family or clan and the religious society or societies to which they belonged. Consequently, disagreements between clans or religious societies almost never posed a serious threat to the basic unity and stability of the Zuni community. ▲

*A Zuni man relaxes at home in this 1890 photograph. Despite the sometimes harsh climate of the Southwest, the Zunis established permanent and fruitful agricultural settlements.*

# 3

# COMMUNITY LIFE

The people of the itiwana made good use of their land. For thousands of years they grew crops, gathered wild plants, and hunted animals. They established small communities, developing strategies that enabled them to thrive in the sometimes harsh environment of the American Southwest.

The Zunis almost always divided work along gender lines. While the Zunis believed that men and women were suited for different tasks, they also believed that gender was more of an acquired than an innate state. Consequently, men who so wished could live as women, wearing women's clothes, performing work traditionally assigned to women, and even taking other men as husbands. Such people were called *lhamana* by the Zunis and were considered a gender distinct from males or females. Family members would sometimes encourage young boys who showed an interest in women's work or in pretending to be women to become lhamanas (women in the family were often especially encouraging; lhamanas were considered especially hard work-

ers and a tremendous help around the house), but the final decision was made by the boy himself when he reached puberty. After a boy decided to become a lhamana, his religious education would continue as though he were a man, but his vocational education would be entirely that of a woman. The lhamana tradition eventually died out in the 20th century due to the rabid opposition of U.S. authorities to the practice.

The work of Zuni men centered on the production of food, and they prepared the land, planted seeds, and harvested crops. Some of these tasks were carried out by individuals, while other work, such as the preparation of fields for planting and the harvesting of crops, was done collectively, usually by a group of relatives.

But the primary difficulty for Zuni farmers was not labor but the water supply. The climate in the Southwest is generally dry, with rainfall averaging only 10 to 15 inches per year. The rain that does fall comes in sudden and severe storms in summer months that can drown or wash away young plants. The only other natural sources of water in the region are the small Zuni River and a few springs. To make the best use of available water, the Zuni farmers developed a system of floodwater irrigation, which involved building small dams and canals with mud walls to direct water from rainfall and overflowing streams to the crops. This method was quite successful, and the Zunis cultivated as many as 10,000 acres of corn, producing a large enough surplus in good years to keep a two-year supply on hand in case of losses from drought or damage caused by insects.

In addition to farming, Zuni men hunted in the surrounding plains, deserts, and mountains. Hunting was

*This 1888 photograph shows We-Wha, a lhamana of great rank, weaving at her loom during a visit to Washington, D.C.*

*Loaves of bread bake in a traditional outdoor oven. The preparation, cooking, and preservation of food were some of the many duties of Zuni women.*

usually done in groups, sometimes as large as 100 or 200 people. Closer to the villages small animals such as rabbits, mice, and other desert rodents were found in abundance, while the more distant woodlands and mountains contained large animals such as deer, antelope, elk, mountain sheep, and bears. Zuni men hunted rabbits with sticks thrown like boomerangs and hunted deer by driving them either into fenced enclosures or into pits dug in the ground, where they could easily be killed.

Zuni men also fished in the Zuni River and its tributaries and snared birds, using delicate traps of wood and twine designed specifically for each species. They trapped eagles, ducks, wild turkeys, hawks, owls, crows, and blue jays, using their flesh for food and their feathers for decorating clothing and ceremonial equipment. In addition to the trapped wild birds, Zuni families kept flocks of domesticated turkeys, which were tended by all household members. These turkeys were raised mainly for their feathers, but when other food was scarce they were also eaten.

Zuni women were responsible for preparing, cooking, and preserving foods. One of their most time-consuming tasks was grinding corn. Many Zuni breads and cakes were made of cornmeal, and it took hours of careful work to produce an adequate amount. Different recipes called for different consistencies of corn meal, ranging from coarse to very fine, and nuts and seeds were ground for food as well. As a result, a Zuni woman owned several grinding stones with varying edges to produce the different types of meal. Once the meal was ground, women would make it into batter to be either fried over a fire or baked in an oven.

Women as well as men grew crops, but only in small gardens generally located along the banks of the Zuni River. These gardens, called waffle gardens because of their distinct appearance, were divided into small square or rectangular cells surrounded by low mud walls that helped to conserve water and protect the plants from wind. Women watered their gardens by hand, using ladles to distribute water that they carried from the Zuni River or from nearby wells. They brought water to gardens in jars called ollas that they carried on their heads.

In addition to growing crops, women gathered many varieties of wild plants growing near their villages. Some of these plants were used for medicinal purposes, such as ointments for burns and eye irritations; painkillers for headaches, toothaches, and sore throats; salves to promote healing of wounds; and drugs to help women in childbirth. Other wild plants, such as nuts, watercress, yucca, juniper berries, sunflowers, wild rice, wild peas, wild potatoes, parsnips, and milkweed, were eaten as supplements to agricultural products and contributed valuable nutrients to people's diet. Because the Zunis relied on their corn and bean crops as their primary source of protein, nuts were especially important as an additional source of protein during crop failures.

Men and women each had specific duties when undertaking tasks such as building a house. The men built the outside structure of houses from sandstone blocks and slabs, then the women plastered the interior walls. The women were responsible for keeping up the plaster, applying fresh coats when the walls deteriorated over time. Women were also responsible for keeping a fire going to heat the houses in winter, but men were responsible for cutting and hauling home the firewood.

Zuni women and men also specialized in different crafts. Women were the potters and were responsible for all stages of the pottery-making process,

*Zuni women tend a waffle garden near the banks of the Zuni River. The distinctive shape of the waffle garden helped conserve irrigation water.*

*A Zuni man drills turquoise in this photograph. Zuni men were responsible for making jewelry and tools, while Zuni women made earthenware.*

from the digging of clay to the final painting. Men made the tools and gear used for farming and hunting, including digging sticks, shovels, axes, bows, and arrows. Men also produced a variety of household utensils and personal items. They made baskets from twined and coiled yucca and rabbitbrush, and they wove the cotton cloth that was fashioned into blankets, clothing, and sashes. Finally, men used turquoise (obtained from the Zunis' mines and quarries, which also produced silver, copper, and obsidian), shell, and coral to craft beautiful jewelry that was worn by all Zunis.

Both men and women wore cotton garments and deerskin- or antelope-hide footwear. Women wore cotton blouses, skirts, and sashes, while men wore cotton shirts, sashes, and aprons over deerskin leggings. Cloth was often dyed with bright mineral or vegetable pigments, and clothing was decorated with embroidered geometric designs.

By skillfully developing their crafts and making good use of their resources, the Zuni lived in prosperity. Their comfortable and secure way of life was described in 1540 by Francisco Vasquez de Coronado, a Spanish officer who led an expedition through the Southwest:

> They have very good homes and good rooms with corridors and some quite good rooms underground and paved, built for the winter. The town of Granada [Coronado's name for the Zuni village Hawikuh] has two hundred houses, all surrounded by a wall. There is another town nearby, but somewhat larger than this, and another of the same size as this; the other four are somewhat smaller.
>
> The people of these towns seem to me to be fairly large and intelligent. They are well built and comely. I think that they have a quantity of turquoises.
>
> The food which they eat consists of maize, of which they have great abundance, beans, and game. They make the best tortillas that I have ever seen anywhere. They have the very best arrangement and method for grinding that was ever seen. They have very good salt in crystals, which they bring from a lake a day's journey distant from here.

The "very good homes" Coronado saw reflected the Zunis' family structure in their architecture. A Zuni house usually had one, two, or three stories of rooms arranged in rows, and related families would occupy a series of adjacent rooms. Zuni families were considered related through the women—married daughters remained in the household into which they were born,

but married sons usually left home and moved into their wife's household. A traditional Zuni household might have included an extended family made up of an elder couple, their daughters, their daughters' husbands and children, and their unmarried sons. This structure weakened the authority of men in the household; consequently, the person who traditionally organized the activities of residents and made sure that all necessary work got done in a Zuni household was the eldest woman. She was also the person to consult for advice concerning problems or major decisions.

In addition to the extended family, the Zuni's social system included kin groups called lineages. A lineage consists of people related by direct descent from a known ancestor or elder. Zuni lineages were matrilineal, or based on the principle of descent through women. The eldest surviving woman in a lineage was usually considered the head of that lineage and played an active role in the lives of its members by giving advice, settling disputes, and organizing group activities. In addition, the head woman would safeguard certain sacred objects that were considered the property of her lineage; these items were usually kept in a bundle placed on an altar erected in a special room of her house. The eldest brother of the head woman was also an important figure in a lineage and would also be consulted by lineage members faced with a conflict or an important decision.

These lineages were combined into larger kinship units called clans. A clan is a grouping of people who believe that they are related by descent from a common ancestor. A member of the more than a dozen Zuni clans could not always trace his or her specific familial relationship to every other member, but clan members believed they were all descendants of a specific figure of the ancient past. As with other Zuni kinship groups, Zuni clans were matrilineal, and Zuni children automatically belonged to the clan of their mother. Nonetheless, the Zuni also had close ties to their father's group, and individuals often referred to themselves as a "child of my father's clan." Clan membership strongly affected people's choice of a marriage partner. Since members of a clan were considered relatives, they could not marry each other. In addition, the Zunis condemned marriages between a person and someone in his or her father's clan.

In addition to their role in determining appropriate marriages, clans served several other functions in Zuni society. Each clan had control over certain areas of farmland within the Zuni territory. The elder women of a clan, who were the clan heads, distributed the land to the lineages and households within their group. Plots of farmland were controlled and could be inherited by the women of an individual household, but these plots were not truly private property belonging to individuals. Rather, land was considered a resource ultimately controlled by the clan as a whole, and members of the clan had the right to use the land according to their needs. Although the women of a household inherited the farmland, the men did the farmwork. A man would work on his mother's land until he married, at which time he would move into his wife's household and work on her family's land.

Because Zuni relatives lived and worked together and shared food and other goods, family members tended to be deeply loyal and emotionally close to each other. Bonds between parents and sons and between sisters and brothers also remained strong even when a man left the household after marriage. Men were expected to frequently return to their first home to help celebrate family occasions and to give aid to their relatives. Indeed, if a man came from an important family that looked after especially sacred objects, he could easily spend more time with (and gain more status from) his own family than his wife's.

The importance of kinship in Zuni life was reflected in people's way of addressing each other. Words used to address close relatives were also used to address other people in the clan. For example, Zunis would call elder women in their clan "mother" and older men in their clan "mother's brother"; older men in their father's clan would be addressed as "father" and older women in their father's clan as "father's sister"; and older people called their younger clan-mates "daughter" or "son." The Zunis used kinship terms for close friends as well. For example, people who were close childhood friends would call each other "brother" or "sister" and each oth-

*Two Zuni men work in a field. Although Zuni men tended the fields and farms of the tribe, the land itself was owned by the women.*

er's parents "mother" and "father." Even certain natural forms merited kinship terms; the earth was "mother" and the sun "father." Rain clouds and fire were called "grandmother," water "grandfather," and corn either "sister" or "brother."

The Zunis formed bonds with non-relatives through marriage. Married couples were expected to act as partners, cooperating in their work and helping to support each other's families. Marriage was seen as a very personal activity, and conduct within a marriage was not regulated by any sort of law (although it could be rich fodder for gossip). Most marriages succeeded, but if a couple did not get along well, either spouse was free to divorce the other (although the woman kept any children). If the man chose to divorce, he simply left his wife's household and returned to his mother's home. If the woman wanted to end the marriage, she put her husband's belongings outside the house, and the man took his possessions and left. But when the marriage succeeded, the bonds it established extended beyond the couple to include both sets of relatives, and children born to the couple could depend upon the members of both their own household and their father's family (or, if their parents divorced, their stepfather's family) for support.

Child-rearing among the Zuni was not only the responsibility of the parent but also of the entire family. Grandparents were often especially indulgent of their grandchildren, instructing and entertaining them by recounting myths and histories of the people. To an extent the entire community was engaged in the raising of each child, because any passer-by was considered free or even obligated to reprimand a misbehaving child. As Zuni children grew up, they gradually learned the tasks that would be required of them as adults. Boys would help their fathers in the fields by planting and weeding crops, while girls would learn to grind corn and would assist their mothers by tending to younger siblings. Zuni children were usually taught by example and encouragement, not by punishment; however, misbehaving children were sometimes told frightening stories about owls, witches, and certain kachinas who carried away naughty children. And if a mother was especially exasperated with her child, she would ask the chief of a kachina society to make sure one of the child-snatching kachinas was present at the next public dance. When the kachina appeared at the dance, it would approach the offending child and menace him, telling him that it was going to carry him off and eat him if he did not behave.

Ideally, Zuni girls and boys would grow up to be generous, helpful, considerate, and moderate people. These characteristics were strongly encouraged and valued by the community. Consequently, visitors to Zuni households were usually given a generous and hospitable welcome. According to Frank Cushing, a researcher who lived with the Zuni for many years in the late 19th century,

The instant greeting to a Zuni house is "Enter, sit, and eat!" Enter any house at whatever time of day or night and the invariable tray of breads will be brought forth, also parched corn, or, if in the seasons, peaches, melons or pinon nuts.

The Zunis strongly disapproved of people who were boastful, argumentative, uncooperative, or stingy. According to Ruth Bunzel, an anthropologist who visited the Zunis from 1928 to 1933,

> In all social relations, whether within the family group or outside, the most honored personality traits are a pleasing address, a yielding disposition, and a generous heart. The person who thirsts for power, who wishes to be, as they scornfully phrase it, "a leader of the people," receives nothing but criticism.

Factionalism and public disagreements were discouraged. Disputes—even those involving fairly serious crimes—were supposed to be settled privately and quietly by the families of the people involved. If a person repeatedly acted in an unacceptable manner, the people in the community would make their disapproval obvious by publicly teasing the wrongdoer (this was often the duty of the ritual clowns) or gossiping about the person's actions to shame the wrongdoer into correcting his or her behavior. Repeated or serious misbehavior exposed a person to accusations of witchcraft, which could lead to ostracism from the tribe or, in extreme cases, execution.

The government of the Zunis consisted of a *pekwin*, who was the head secular authority, and a council of priests, who were responsible for managing collective work, community affairs, and religious ceremonies. Each village had its own pekwin and council. The pekwin was named to the position by a council of priests and could be removed from office by that same council if the people disapproved of his behavior. To become a pekwin, a man had to have a generous and kind disposition and to be respected by all; in addition, he had to be a member of the Dogwood clan. The pekwin was officially installed in office during a ceremony conducted by the head Rain Priest of the village, who would place a staff made of feathers in the chief's hands, recite a prayer, and then blow on the staff four times.

The council of priests appointed a pekwin to govern because it believed that if the priests became directly involved in village disputes, they would no longer be pure of heart, and their prayers would lose power. Priests nonetheless exercised a great deal of influence in the villages by setting moral examples and encouraging others to act properly. To help with the more practical problems of governance, the pekwin had two assistants who were warriors and members of the Bow Priesthood.

Thanks to a unique system of government, a thorough exploitation of the resources around them, and a social system that emphasized mutual support and cooperation, the Zuni created a

*A group of Bow Priests (including ethnologist and adopted Zuni Frank Cushing) perform a ceremony. Bow Priests were responsible for carrying out the day-to-day duties of governance.*

smoothly functioning society that provided most individuals with lives of security and purpose. Even the Spanish conquistadores who came into Zuni territory in the early 16th century remarked on the orderliness and fellowship that marked Zuni society. One soldier, named Castaneda, wrote in 1540,

> They have priests who preach; these are aged men who ascend to the highest terrace of the village and deliver a sermon at sunrise. The people sit around and listen in profound silence. These old men give them advice in regard to their manner of living, which they think it their duty to observe; for there is no drunkenness among them, no unnatural vice; there are no thieves; on the contrary, they are very laborious.

The Zunis prospered through the centuries by developing their resources and living for the most part in harmony with the people around them. But their stability was threatened in the 16th century when invaders from Spain came into the American Southwest looking for treasures and remained there to dominate the original inhabitants. ▲

*Antonio de Mendoza, the first viceroy of Mexico, sent out expeditions to the American Southwest in hopes of discovering and conquering wealthy tribes of Native Americans.*

# DEFENDING
# THE
# HOMELAND

The Spanish invasion of the Southwest began in the early years of the 16th century. The Spanish had defeated the rich Aztec empire in central Mexico in 1521 and were seeking to extend their control over other, hopefully equally wealthy Native American tribes. Spanish explorers traveled through the northern provinces of Mexico, searching for cities filled with treasures but finding only small groups of farmers, hunters, and gatherers. Eventually the explorers mounted expeditions into the territory of the Zunis and other Pueblo tribes. Accompanying these explorers were priests belonging to the Franciscan order of the Catholic church, who hoped to convert the Native Americans to Christianity.

In 1538 the viceroy of Mexico, Antonio de Mendoza, chose a Franciscan priest named Fray Marcos de Niza to lead a party into present-day New Mexico and Arizona. The viceroy wanted to gain subjects for the king of Spain and converts for the Catholic church. He told Niza,

You must explain to the natives of the land that there is only one God in heaven, and the Emperor on earth to rule and govern it, whose subjects they all must become and whom they must serve.

Marcos de Niza ventured into the American Southwest early in 1539, sending a small group in advance of the main contingent under the leadership of a Moor named Esteban. Esteban's party reached Zuni lands, but once they arrived, Esteban gravely offended the tribe and was executed. Esteban's specific offense is not known—according to Zuni oral tradition, the "black Mexican" was "greedy, voracious and bold"—but some have speculated that he unwisely informed the Zunis of the size and military nature of the larger party that was to join him.

In any case, when word of Esteban's death reached Niza, he quickly returned to Mexico and told Viceroy Mendoza that he had found a kingdom richer even than the empire of the Aztecs. It is unclear whether Niza actually saw Hawikuh during his expedition; in any case, he wildly exaggerated its wealth, claiming that its houses were decorated with turquoise and other jewels. Niza also claimed that Hawikuh formed a part of a mighty empire called the Seven Cities of Cibola, and the territory of the Zunis was known as Cibola (probably a corruption of the Zuni phrase *Shi-wi-na*, used to indicate any permanent Zuni town or residence) and the Zunis themselves as Cibolans for years to come. Niza's fertile imagination was reflected in his name for the Cibolan empire; the Zunis probably inhabited only six villages at this time, but both Aztec and European legend mentioned wealthy empires encompassing seven cities, so Niza credited the Zunis with seven.

Obviously, news of the Seven Cities of Cibola was quite welcome to Viceroy Mendoza, who sent a large force into the region to conquer the wealthy Cibolans and plunder their treasures. The expedition—consisting of 230 soldiers on horseback, 70 foot soldiers, several Franciscan priests, and hundreds of Mexican Indians—was led by Francisco Vasquez de Coronado. Coronado planned to force the Cibolans to submit to Spain's authority, while the Franciscans planned to establish missions and convert the empire of Cibola to Christianity.

The Zunis, of course, had their own plans. Expecting reprisals for the killing of Esteban, the Zunis prepared for an attack at Hawikuh, evacuating all women, children, and elderly from the village onto nearby mesas. The Zunis made a preliminary attempt to drive off the Spanish by attacking them at a narrow canyon near the juncture of the Zuni and Little Colorado rivers, and they inflicted several casualties. But the Spanish continued toward Hawikuh, reaching an open plain south of town in early July 1540. According to a Spanish officer, when the Spanish arrived at the plain, they "found all the Indians of Cibola and the people of other places who had gathered to meet us with force."

Six hundred Zuni warriors were assembled to turn back the Spanish invasion. At first the battle went well for the Zunis, who managed to repel the initial Spanish assault, but the superior weaponry of the Spanish helped turn the tide, and when the soldiers began a second attack against Hawikuh, the Zunis, suffering serious casualties, surrendered the town. Coronado, who had been injured in the battle, and his men occupied Hawikuh. The village proved to be somewhat disappointing to the Spanish: most of the residents had fled, and Hawikuh lacked the lavish riches reported by Niza. The conquistadores were quite impressed with the Zunis' agricultural bounty, but they were in search of gold, not grain, and eventually left Zuni territory to investigate the villages of the Pueblo tribes along the Rio Grande River. Several priests and soldiers stayed behind for another two years to assert Spanish authority in the region; they returned to Mexico in 1542, leaving two Mexican Indian converts to Christianity to spread the word among the Zunis. According to a Spanish officer

*Francisco Vasquez de Coronado led a sizable army into the American Southwest in search of gold and treasures. Although his expedition was a military success, it failed in its mercenary goal.*

*Zuni warriors attempt to defend Hawikuh from the Spanish advance. Although the Zunis repelled the initial attack, the superior weapons technology of the Spanish proved decisive, and the conquistadores took the village.*

who was a member of the party traveling to Mexico, after they left Hawikuh, "For two or three days, the Zunis never ceased to follow the rear guard of the army to pick up any baggage or Indian servants . . . they rejoiced at keeping some of our people."

Although the party of priests and soldiers was harassed by Zuni warriors, the two Mexican Indians left behind were treated quite well and, according to later visitors to Hawikuh, eventually recanted their Christianity and married into the tribe. This pattern was to be repeated throughout the period of Span-

ish conquest; the Zuni tradition of generosity and hospitality to strangers resulted in most visitors being treated quite well, but newcomers who attempted to disrupt or interfere with traditional Zuni life were threatened, harassed, or killed.

After Coronado left Zuni territory in 1540, he set up headquarters in the Pueblo village of Tiguex, located on the Rio Grande near present-day Bernadillo, New Mexico. From there he sent expeditions to contact and to obtain tribute from other Pueblo villages, eventually exercising dominion over nearly all the

Rio Grande villages. The Zunis, however, were located far to the west of the Rio Grande, and after Coronado's disappointment the Spanish had little interest in exploiting their territory. As a result, for the next 40 years the Zunis had no recorded contact with the Spanish, although informal meetings may have occurred, and the Zunis almost certainly obtained information on Spanish activities through their trade with the other Pueblo tribes.

In 1581 the Spanish, in an attempt to both enlarge their domain and investigate persistent rumors of incredible treasure to the west, sent an expedition into Zuni territory led by Francisco Sanchez Chamuscado, but the only riches he found were agricultural. Two years later Antonio de Espejo led a contingent to the Zuni village of Matsaki, looking for copper and silver mines. He failed to find the mines and soon departed from the area, but he left behind several soldiers and priests in the area to codify Spanish control.

As with Coronado, the Zunis benefited immensely in their dealings with Espejo by being in an out-of-the-way location that was not believed to contain anything of great value. Espejo and his soldiers routinely demanded vast quantities of food and clothing from the Pueblo Indians who lived along the Rio Grande, and they usually slaughtered the inhabitants of any village that defied them. Because of their location the Zunis escaped much of this mistreatment, but the combination of deference and defensive preparation that marked their future relations with the Spanish strongly indicates that they had heard tales of the repeated atrocities.

In 1598 the Spanish government established a permanent colony of settlers in what was called New Mexico and named Juan de Oñate as the first governor of the colony. Oñate was determined to exploit both the human and mineral resources of the colony, and he traveled to the territory of the Zunis in the year of his appointment to order the Zuni leaders to declare their obedience to the Spanish king and to explore their territory for natural resources of value. Of special interest to Oñate were the rumored copper mines of the Zunis and Zuni Salt Lake, which could provide settlers with a popular seasoning and preservative. Oñate sent two parties of soldiers to explore and assess these potential sources of wealth. The soldiers sent to the mines reported that they had indeed found mines of great antiquity, but they were vague as to both the location and the potential value of the excavations. The soldiers sent to Zuni Salt Lake were more encouraging, reporting that the lake had a crust of salt on it so thick that a man could walk on it, and bringing back a sample of salt that Oñate declared superior to any found in Europe.

Oñate hardly left the area encouraged, however. As useful as a salt lake might be for supporting a settlement, it was hardly the literal gold mine he had hoped to find. Oñate's search for exploitable resources reached a head as complaints about his conduct led to threats that he would lose the governorship of New Mexico. He visited Zuni territory again in 1604, looking for the copper mines his men had supposedly located on the earlier expedition. A Spanish official who accompanied the expedition noted that four of the six Zuni villages were "almost completely in ruins," a fact that probably reflects the toll taken by European diseases as well as the migrations caused by intermittent conflicts with passing Spanish soldiers.

Oñate's second search for the Zuni mines was a failure, and in 1607 authorities in Mexico removed him as governor of the colony and replaced him with Pedro de Peralta, who arrived in 1609 and established a provincial capital in the village of Santa Fe. Peralta, however, continued the abusive policies of his predecessors, exacting forced labor and tribute from the Rio Grande Pueblo Indians. The Franciscan missionaries also became quite powerful during this period and were equally brutal in their exploitation of the Native Americans. Missionaries forced the Pueblo Indians to work in their fields and homes, to build churches and houses in their villages, and to attend church services. In addition, many missionaries destroyed non-Christian ceremonial objects and religious works of art, and they punished defiant or uncooperative Native Americans with public whippings, tortures, and executions. Native Americans who practiced their traditional religions were often viciously persecuted for practicing witchcraft, a crime defined by the Spanish as any exercise of non-Christian reli-

gious activities.

Once again the location of the Zunis' settlements allowed them to escape some of the more intense forms of control, but their experience with Spanish missionaries was negative enough that Spanish-speaking Catholics were banned from Zuni rituals and dances well into the 20th century. The missionaries to the Zunis usually served a large area and never stayed long in any one village. As a result the Zunis would usually abstain from their public religious ceremonies when a missionary was in town, then continue as usual once the missionary left.

The Zunis were no more cooperative with the secular Spanish authorities. The Zunis were expected to pay tribute and to perform work for Spanish authorities, including farmwork and the gathering of piñon nuts, which were sold by officials for huge profits in Mexico. But the Spanish soon discovered that the Zunis would only pay tribute when threatened by an armed force, an expensive, tiresome, and not altogether safe way to make collections. Officials in Santa Fe eventually gave up on collecting tribute from the Zuni after 1621.

Eventually the Spanish tried to reassert control over the Zunis. In the late 1620s an officer named Silva Nieto led a contingent of 30 soldiers and several priests into Zuni lands. Nieto demanded that the people submit to Spanish authority, but the Zunis, led by their council of religious elders, refused. Nieto departed but left two Franciscan priests to establish a mission in the vil-

*A European engraving illustrates the cruelty of the Spanish conquistadores toward the Native Americans. Among the Pueblo Indians, the Spanish instituted programs of forced labor, tribute, and religious conversion that caused tremendous hardship.*

*Dowa Yallane looms in the background of this 1879 photograph. The easily defended mesa provided the Zunis with needed sanctuary during their various conflicts with the Spanish.*

lage of Hawikuh. The presence of the priests was an immediate source of conflict, and Nieto had to return with his soldiers a few days after leaving to menace the Zunis into accepting them.

The priests—the first permanent resident missionaries in Zuni territory—were quick to begin what they considered the work of God. Using Zuni labor, they oversaw the construction of a mission compound in Hawikuh, which con-

tained a massive church with a nave measuring 103 feet by 20 feet as well as a kitchen, a chapel, residences, and workrooms. The compound was completed in 1632, and a second mission was established in the town of Halona at about the same time.

The Franciscan missionaries may have felt optimistic, but they had seriously underestimated the resentment caused by their use of Zuni labor and their interference with Zuni religious life. This resentment was worsened after a new priest—a blunt, opinionated, and unpopular man—arrived in Hawikuh determined to stamp out the Zunis' religion. Shortly after the compounds were built, the new priest attempted to interfere with a Zuni ceremony and force those in attendance to go to mass instead. The Zunis, infuriated at his audacity, killed him and another priest who was passing through the area and destroyed the missions. The other resident priests immediately vacated the territory, and officials in Santa Fe sent soldiers to punish the people responsible.

By the time the soldiers reached the Zuni villages, however, the Zunis had abandoned them and settled in a large community on top of an easily defended mesa called Dowa Yallane, or Corn Mountain. The Zunis eventually allowed some missionaries accompanying the soldiers into their new village to negotiate a settlement. The Zunis promised to accept the authority of the Spanish crown, and the Spanish promised to allow the Zunis to return to their villages. The Spanish soldiers left the region, but the cautious Zunis remained on Dowa Yallane for another three years before returning to their old villages.

The lack of Spanish documentation concerning the Zunis from 1632 to 1680 seems to indicate that authorities made few additional attempts to control them at this time, although informal contact almost surely continued. A few missionaries took up residence in Zuni towns and attempted, with little success, to have the Zunis rebuild the missions. The missionaries did have some impact on Zuni life, however; when the Zunis publicly performed their traditional religious dances and ceremonies, the priests reportedly arrested a number of the religious leaders and punished them with public beatings, as well as by confiscating ritual objects and burning kivas. Despite what was surely bad blood between the missionaries and Zunis, only one missionary was reported as having been murdered during this period, and he was apparently the victim of Navajo or Apache raiders.

Resentment ran high against the Spanish nonetheless. In 1680 the Zunis joined a Pueblo Indian conspiracy, led by a Tewa named Popé, to oust the Spanish officials, soldiers, priests, and settlers from the Southwest. Popé and the other leaders planned a siege of the provincial capital of Santa Fe. They decided to start their rebellion in the summer, just before an annual delivery of supplies from Mexico, when the Spanish would have the fewest guns and ammunition. August 11, 1680, was set as the date for the rebellion, and two messengers were chosen to travel to all the towns and convey details of the planned uprising to all the Pueblo tribes. But the Spanish governor, Antonio de Otermin, found out about the impending revolt and arrested the two messengers on August 9. When word of the arrests spread in the villages, the leaders decided to begin the rebellion immediately. The Pueblo Revolt began on August 10, when the

*This message, carved into a large rock (now called Inscription Rock, located at the El Morro National Monument in New Mexico) by a member of the expedition sent to reconquer the Pueblo Indians, reads "Here was the general Don Diego de Vargas who conquered for our faith and Royal Crown all of New Mexico at his own expense in the year 1692."*

inhabitants of the Rio Grande villages cut off water and supplies to Santa Fe, and by August 21 all Spanish troops and settlers had left the Southwest.

The Zunis carried out their part of the Pueblo Revolt by killing the resident priest of Halona (according to Zuni oral tradition, another priest was allowed to live because he disavowed his Christianity and became a Zuni), burning the church buildings that they had been forced to build, and expelling Spanish settlers who had intruded on their land.

As a defensive measure, the Zunis once again abandoned their villages and moved to a settlement on top of Dowa Yallane, where they remained for over 15 years.

In 1692 a Spanish commander named Diego de Vargas led a large force of soldiers from Mexico into Pueblo territory and regained control of most of the towns along the Rio Grande. Vargas traveled west to reconquer the Hopis and the Zunis. When he reached Dowa Yallane, he was received with surprising cordiality by the Zunis. Although Zuni leaders had met with representatives from the nearby Hopis and Keres in order to plan a united defense against the Spanish, the size of the Spanish force that reached Dowa Yallane probably compelled the Zuni leadership to offer instead to live in peace with the intruders. In addition, after the Pueblo Revolt the Zunis had had increasing trouble with raiders from other Native American tribes. The introduction of the horse to America had made the formerly peaceful Navajos and Apaches fearsome foes who could raid a farm, steal crops, livestock, and people, and escape with lightning speed. Comanche and Ute raiders had also moved into the area. The powerful Spanish military probably made a tempting prospect to the Zunis as an ally against the raiders.

But the Zunis had not completely capitulated to the Spanish. When in 1694 another Spanish contingent approached Dowa Yallane seeking tribute and oaths of obedience, the Zuni successfully fought off the soldiers, inflicting many casualties and causing the army to quickly retreat to Santa Fe. This successful resistance led to rumors in Santa Fe that the Zunis and their allies among the Hopis, Keres, and Apaches planned to attack Spanish settlements. Missionaries added to the tension by complaining that the Zunis refused to convert to Christianity. The missionaries finally formally requested that Diego de Vargas, the governor at Santa Fe, send soldiers against the Zunis, but Vargas believed the rumors to be false and denied the request. The armed uprising never materialized.

The Spanish nonetheless continued to seek obedience from the Zunis. In 1699 a new governor, Pedro Rodriguez Cubero, sent a delegation to Dowa Yallane in order to have the Zunis renew earlier pledges of peace. The meeting seems to have gone fairly well, for shortly after the Spanish delegation left, the Zunis finally moved down from their defensive settlement on Dowa Yallane. The threat of attacks from both raiders and the Spanish still existed, however, and the Zunis concentrated their population in the town of Halona (later called Zuni by English-speaking Americans), on the assumption that it would be easier to defend one large village than several small settlements scattered over a wide area.

As the defensive design of Halona suggests, although the Zunis had agreed not to fight against the Spanish, they were far from being conquered or even reconquered. Despite tremendous pressure from their would-be conquistadores, the Zunis never acquiesced to foreign control of their government, and at the end of the 17th century they remained a free and independent people. ▲

*A Zuni man mounts a ladder to enter a house in this 1900 photograph. This distinctive means of entry and exit was created in response to the repeated military threats of Spanish soldiers and Native American raiders.*

# ALIENS ON NATIVE SOIL

As the 18th century began, the Spanish continued their attempts to increase their authority over the Pueblo Indians. Although they were able to govern the people living in villages along the Rio Grande with relative ease, they had difficulty controlling the Zunis. Since the Zunis lived far from Santa Fe, officials found it too costly to continually send troops to force them to comply with Spanish laws. The Zunis' isolation from the Spanish domain was aided by the fact that Navajos and Apaches inhabited the territory between the Zunis and the Rio Grande. These tribes routinely raided soldiers on the march, and Spanish officials quickly became reluctant to risk troops and supplies by sending them through this dangerous territory to the Zunis.

On the rare occasions that the Spanish visited the Zunis, the Zuni leaders would readily promise to live in peace with the Spanish, to follow Spanish law, to attend Catholic services, and to give up their traditional religious practices. As soon as the authorities returned to Santa Fe, however, the Zunis would ignore all requests for tribute and resume their religious practices. As a result, of the three missions built in Zuni villages by the middle of the 17th century, only one, a church at Halona, was rebuilt after the reconquest, and it was seldom used.

Not surprisingly, Franciscan missionaries made only a few permanent converts among the Zunis and other Pueblo Indians. Indeed, although missionaries became a regular sight in Halona, they were usually visiting from other Pueblo villages, and more frequently acted as diplomats than religious leaders. In 1776 a priest named Fray Dominguez wrote about the mission's lack of success:

> Even at the end of so many years since the reconquest, . . . their condition

now is almost the same as it was in the beginning, for generally speaking they have preserved some very indecent, and perhaps superstitious customs.

Their repugnance and resistance to most Christian acts is evident, for they perform the duties pertaining to the Church under compulsion, and there are usually many omissions.

In addition to the resistance of the Native Americans themselves, friction between Spanish civil and religious authorities helped the Zunis maintain their isolation and independence. Civilian officials often complained about the lack of progress made by Franciscans among the Pueblo Indians and noted the priests' abusive and illegal practices. Juan Antonio de Ornedal y Masa, an envoy of the Spanish viceroy, listed several improprieties:

> The religious almost totally neglect the Indians, even failing to say mass for them. The missionaries, in violation of the law, fail to learn the Native language and to teach the Indians the Spanish language. The missionaries forcibly take grain and sheep from the Indians who are also compelled to weave for them wool and cotton without pay. They arbitrarily take from the Indians buffalo skins that they obtain for sheltering themselves and the buckskins that they sell. When the Indians complain of this to the civil authorities, the priests threaten them with whippings and other punishments.

For their part, missionaries repeatedly wrote to the viceroy and recounted abuses by civil authorities against the Pueblo Indians. In 1761 Fray Pedro Serrano complained that officials forced men, women, and children to weave blankets, harvest corn, and perform domestic work. Serrano ended his letter by observing that

> These officials never conduct themselves in any way that yields any benefit to the Indians. . . . We religious suffer many injuries, outrages, and afflictions from the officials if we try to defend the unfortunate Indians in any way. . . . The officials laugh, for they alone are favored and protected [knowing that] the best officials are those who oppress the Indians most.

As a result of the bickering, resistance, and general lack of missionary success, the Franciscans had all but stopped their missionary activity among the Zunis when they were officially recalled by the newly formed Mexican government in 1821.

Although the Zunis never abandoned their own religious and cultural practices, the Zunis and the Spanish did cooperate in some areas. The Zunis generally accepted the presence of priests in their towns and, in keeping with their traditional ideal of generous hospitality toward strangers, even warmly welcomed missionaries and other Spanish visitors. However, if the actions of newcomers violated Zuni norms, the offenders were dealt with decisively. For example, in 1700 a group of Spanish sol-

*Zuni men work metal in a smithy. Although the Zunis had limited contacts with the Spanish, the Spanish did introduce them to new technologies such as blacksmithing.*

diers, accompanied by a missionary and three Spanish settlers, were welcomed into Halona to defend the village against raiders. But the troops and settlers treated the Zunis with disdain and curtness, and behaved licentiously toward the Zuni women. On March 3, 1703, the Zunis decided that they had had enough and killed the three settlers, sparing the missionary because he had behaved well and the soldiers only because they were absent from town that day. The Zunis did not believe that the killings would go unpunished and quickly evacuated once again to Dowa Yallane, but the Spanish had decided by this point that the survival of their colonists depended upon the cultivation of goodwill among the Pueblo Indians. Consequently, the

Spanish expedition sent to Dowa Yallane two years later was led by the spared missionary, who made an agreement with the Zunis promising them clemency and military protection. The Zunis promptly moved back to Halona and even sent delegates to a 1706 meeting in Santa Fe between the new Spanish governor and representatives of all the Pueblo tribes (except the militantly anti-Spanish Hopis, who eventually engaged in some minor conflicts with the Zunis because of the latter's cooperation with the Spanish).

After the 1705 agreement, the Zunis even engaged in a temporary military alliance with the Spanish. Throughout the 18th century, the Navajos and Apaches carried out several attacks

*A Zuni man uses a burro to carry a large load of firewood. Burros, introduced to the American continents by the Spanish, profoundly affected Zuni living patterns, making possible the habitation of outlying farm settlements.*

against the village of Halona, with casualties resulting on both sides. In retaliation, Zuni warriors sometimes joined Spanish soldiers in expeditions against the Navajos and Apaches. These joint actions did not, however, create a lasting alliance or bond between the Zunis and Spanish but were rather merely a temporary expedience for the beleaguered and vengeful Zunis. Indeed, by the late 18th century Spanish authorities had given up hope of dominating the Zunis and other western Pueblo Indians, and in 1799 only seven Spanish people were recorded as living among the Zunis. Spanish rule in all of the American Southwest finally ended in 1821, when the nation of Mexico won its independence from Spain.

Although the Zuni had remained mostly independent during the period of Spanish domination, contact with these foreigners had affected their lives in several important ways. They adopted numerous articles of European manufacture, such as metal knives, axes, saws, scissors, nails, pots, and kettles. These metal implements and utensils were more durable than traditional wooden, bone, or clay items.

The Spanish also introduced a number of new crops to the Zunis that had been brought either from Europe or from Mexico, such as wheat, oats, peaches, apples, melons, tomatoes, and chili. In addition, the Spanish introduced the Zunis to sheep and burros, animals that would greatly alter the Zuni economy. Burros were useful as pack animals, while sheep were valuable sources of both meat and wool. Zuni women spun the wool into yarn and wove it into blankets and clothing, which were sold to Spanish and Mexican traders.

An indirect but profound result of the Spanish invasion was a change in Zuni settlement patterns. Before 1540 the Zunis resided in six villages along the Zuni River, but by the end of the 16th century all but one of these villages, Halona (later Zuni) had been abandoned. Due to the large increase in the number of residents in this village, a great deal of new housing was constructed. Rooms were added to existing houses, and new homes were built on hills facing the Zuni River as well as on flat ground at the edge of the village.

Because of the circumstances under which Halona was expanded, the new buildings changed Halona's design so that it was better suited for military defense. The large, multistoried houses of the village all faced inward around central plazas, which were only accessible through a few narrow passages. Rooms on the ground floor usually had no doors or windows, and to enter a house, a person had to climb up a ladder onto the rooftop and then climb down another ladder through an entrance in the roof. If intruders approached the village, the ladders to rooftops could be pulled up, barring access to the rooms and their inhabitants below.

The crops and animals introduced by the Spanish also affected settlement patterns. Once people owned large numbers of sheep, they needed to devote a good deal of time to grazing the animals and had to turn part of their land into pasture for sheep. At the same time, the introduction of the burro meant that fairly large amounts of produce or supplies could be easily carried long distances from a field to the village or vice versa. As a result of these two developments, in the early 18th century the Zuni established several small farming communities and herding camps a substantial distance from Halona. At first these communities and camps were inhabited only during the summer, but three of the communities became permanent later in the century. The village farthest from Halona was called Nutria (or *toya* in Zuni) and was located 25 miles northeast of Halona along the Nutria River. Ojo Caliente (or *kapkwayina*, meaning "water comes up from the depths") was established 15 miles to the southwest of Halona, and Pescado (or *heshota cina*, meaning "marked house") was situated east of Halona on the Pescado River.

Yet another change that occurred during the period of Spanish influence was the establishment of civilian government in Zuni villages. Prior to the Spanish invasion, religious leaders governed the towns through their appointment of a pekwin. After the reconquest of 1692, the Spanish set up a council of civil authorities that operated as a parallel council to the traditional leadership, which retained control over religious and moral matters. The civilian government included a governor, a lieutenant governor, and a village council. At first the Spanish appointed the head of the Bow Priesthood as governor, but by the

middle of the 19th century the governor, lieutenant governor, and councillors were chosen by Zuni religious elders. Although civilian and religious leaders had separate duties, they were installed in office through similar ceremonies. The head of the Rain Priesthood installed the traditional pekwin and also gave the oath of office to the civil governor. And just as the pekwin received a ceremonial staff of feathers as a symbol of his office, the civilian governor was given a wooden cane as his symbol of office.

Finally, a tragic result of contact between the Zuni and the Spanish was the introduction of deadly diseases of European origin. Before Europeans arrived in North America, the organisms that cause smallpox, measles, and influenza did not exist on the continent. Since the Zunis and other Native Americans had never been exposed to these diseases, they had not developed any natural resistances or immunities to them. Consequently, when the organisms were brought to America by the Europeans, they spread quickly and with deadly force among the vulnerable indigenous population.

Throughout North America, millions of Native Americans died during widespread epidemics that erupted soon after contact with Europeans. The Zunis were no exception, and several devastating epidemics of smallpox and measles struck Zuni communities in the 16th and 17th centuries. Although population figures for the early years of the Spanish invasion are not completely reliable, the

*Two Navajo men ride horseback through the Southwest. Navajo and Apache raiders attacked and harassed Zuni settlements throughout the 18th and 19th centuries.*

Zuni population may have been as high as 10,000 in the mid–16th century. By the time of the Pueblo Revolt in 1680, their population had declined to 2,500. The population decreases continued, and by the end of the 18th century the Zuni numbered only 1,600. Their population did not begin to increase again until late in the 19th century.

When the Spanish left the Southwest in 1821, the Mexican government assumed jurisdiction over the region. The government declared that Native Americans were full citizens of Mexico and that their rights as citizens would be protected. But the Mexican authorities had no effective contact with the Zunis and other Pueblo Indians, who lived in what was then a marginal, outlying province of a new nation. This proved beneficial to the Zunis, who were able to practice their traditions free from official interference or harassment.

Even before the Mexican government gained control in the Southwest, however, intruders from the United States began to enter Zuni territory. A Creole trader named Baptiste Lalande arrived in the Southwest in 1804, followed in 1821 by William Becknell, who set up trading operations in Santa Fe. Shortly afterward American fur trappers entered the region, purchasing food and supplies from the Native Americans. Such commerce between Mexican citizens and foreigners was illegal under Mexican laws, but American merchants, attracted to Halona's reputation as a center for intertribal trade, tried to establish trade networks with the Zunis. But

because the Americans were primarily interested in valuable beaver furs and the supply of beavers in the Southwest was very small, trade between the Zunis and Americans was not particularly profitable, and by 1835 most of the American traders had left the region.

Mexican jurisdiction over the Southwest was threatened with the outbreak of the Mexican War between the United States and Mexico in the mid-1840s. In addition to fighting with the Mexicans, U.S. troops in the Southwest fought a number of battles with Navajo raiders. In 1846, while in pursuit of some Navajo horse thieves, a group of about 60 U.S. soldiers happened upon the Zuni village. The Zunis were delighted to find a common enemy of the Navajos, and the tribe fed and housed the soldiers in a most congenial manner. A report of the encounter between the Zunis and Americans, written by a private in the army unit involved, noted:

> As soon as our horses were unsaddled, [the Zunis] furnished us with a house, and took us all off to different houses to eat. I went to one house where they set out a soup made with mutton and various kinds of vegetables, and a kind of bread as thin as paper. They have the reputation of being the most hospitable people in the world, which I believe they merit in every respect.
>
> We were out of provision and proposed to buy from them but they said they did not sell their provisions and more particularly to Americans. So they brought in

*(continued on page 81)*

# BELONGING
## TO
## THE
## ZUNI

Zuni artists have been painting for hundreds of years—1,000-year-old pictographs made from earth pigments can still be found in the region surrounding Zuni, New Mexico. Contemporary painting has changed a great deal from the traditional forms; the brighter colors of commercially available paints have replaced earth tones, and newer paintings usually include landscape backgrounds and a level of detail not found in the older works.

Although many modern Zuni artists make jewelry or fetishes for financial reasons, Zuni painters are currently gaining new respect and a wider audience. To celebrate the continuing legacy of Zuni painting, in 1994 the A:shiwi A:wan Museum and Heritage Center (colons indicate glottal stops) collaborated with the University of New Mexico Art Museum to display a show entitled A:shiwi A:wan/Belonging to the Zuni, which featured the works of eight contemporary Zuni artists: Filbert Bowannie, Ronnie Cachini, Duane Dishta, Phil Hughte, Chris Natachu, Eldred Sanchez, Patrick Sanchez, and Alex Seowtewa. Some of the paintings from this show appear on these pages.

Chris Natachu. Untitled (n.d.). Acrylic on rag paper.

*Ronnie Cachini.* Buffalo Dancer *(1993). Acrylic on canvas.*

*Eldred Sanchez. Untitled (1982). Acrylic on canvas.*

*Duane Dishta.* Deer Dance *(1993).* Acrylic on canvas.

*Alex Seowtewa.* Shalako *(1986). Mixed media.*

*Filbert Bowannie. Untitled (n.d.). Watercolor on board.*

*Phil Hughte.* Delay of Game *(n.d.). Acrylic on canvas.*

*Patrick Sanchez.* Splendor of Zuni *(n.d.). Acrylic on canvas board.*

(continued from page 72)

sufficient bread and meal to last our party into camp, which is three days from here. Our saddles, bridles, and all equipment was left exposed to them, but in the morning, not a single article was gone. Where can such a mass of honest people be found?

The cordial meeting was climaxed with an exchange of official pledges of peace and friendship between the army officers and the Zuni governor Lai-iu-ah-tsai-ah.

The Mexican War ended with Mexico's defeat in 1848. The Treaty of Guadalupe Hidalgo, signed by both countries after the war, granted the United States possession of the present-day states of New Mexico and Arizona. The treaty also contained a clause wherein the American government promised to respect the land and rights of the indigenous inhabitants of its new possession. That same year, Lai-iu-ah-tsai-ah and other Zuni leaders met with Navajo leaders and U.S. Army Lieutenant Colonel Henderson P. Boyakin to sign a three-way peace treaty between the Zunis, Navajos, and Americans. The treaty stated in part that the Zunis "shall be protected in the full management of all their rights of Private Property and Religion . . . [by] the authorities, civil and military, of New Mexico and the United States."

By the middle of the 19th century the Zunis had been exposed to three foreign governments, each with its own plans for the indigenous peoples. Despite the

General A. W. Doniphan, one of the commanding officers of the U.S. Army battalion that happened upon the Zunis in1846.

turnover in outside powers, the Zunis had managed to maintain their own security and continue their traditional way of living, and when faced with a new would-be overlord, they had obtained treaties and agreements that explicitly protected their rights and properties. But the government, people, and traditions of the United States would put entirely new pressures on Zuni society, pressures that no treaty could contain. ▲

*A wagon train camped near Santa Fe, New Mexico, in 1880. American settlers, both those intending to settle near Zuni territory and those simply passing through, created a host of problems for the tribe.*

# LOSSES
## AND
# RECOVERIES

One year after the United States signed a treaty with the Zunis, the tribe was visited by the superintendent of Indian affairs for the area, James Calhoun. Calhoun expressed his desire to maintain friendly relations with the Zunis, and the Zuni leaders expressed their hope of living in peace. The friendly relations between the two governments were further cemented in 1863, when President Abraham Lincoln presented the Zuni governor, Mariano, with a silver-knobbed ebony cane, which thereafter became the ceremonial cane of office.

But relations were far from ideal. The discovery of gold in California in 1850 brought a stream of travelers across Zuni lands. Most of these people were just passing through on their way to California, but some of them stole crops and livestock from Zuni farms. In addition, a number of people stayed in the area, enough so that the U.S. Congress organized the area as the Territory of New Mexico in 1850.

The 1850s also saw several expeditions of scientists and technicians sent by the U.S. government to conduct geographic surveys of New Mexico. A researcher named Baldwin Mollhausen described the Zunis' prosperity at the time. He wrote,

> They breed sheep, keep horses and asses, and practice agriculture on an extensive scale. In all directions, fields of wheat and maize, as well as gourds and melons, bore testimony to their industry. In gardens, they raise beans and onions. And the women are skillful in the art of weaving, and manufacture durable blankets.

These expeditions were not sent out to observe the Zunis, however, but to find feasible land routes to California. A road linking New Mexico with southern California was quickly built that passed near Zuni; since the towns and forts that sprung up near the tribe were the first American settlements of any size east of Los Angeles, the Zunis began to see more and more travelers who stopped in the area to get provisions.

Other expeditions *were* sent by the U.S. government for the sole purpose of observing the Zunis and other Pueblo Indians. Beginning in the 1870s, the U.S. Bureau of American Ethnology sent teams to contact Native Americans in the region and study their societies. The writings of these ethnologists excited a great deal of national attention, and as a result increasing numbers of white American tourists began to visit Zuni territory. But the American ethnologists did not simply write about the Zunis, they also took material artifacts of Zuni culture, such as pots, prayer sticks, and masks, to send or sell to museums. The sheer scale of some of these collecting expeditions—in 1881 one team alone shipped over 3,700 items of Zuni manufacture and over 3,000 items of Hopi manufacture to the Smithsonian National Museum in Washington, D.C.—rendered them comparable to the early Spanish tribute-collecting expeditions. Some of these items were purchased from willing sellers, but many were sacred items that were simply seized or stolen from the tribe.

During the 1870s increasing numbers of American missionaries arrived in the area with the purpose of converting the Zunis to various sects of Christianity. A group of Mormon missionaries founded a permanent settlement on the boundary of Zuni territory in 1876, and in response the Presbyterians built a mission and school just north of Zuni the following year. Neither sect met with much success: during this time Mormons were viewed with suspicion and hostility by U.S. authorities, who actively discouraged the Zunis from becoming Mormons, and few Zuni parents wanted the foreigners at the Presbyterian school to supervise their children's education (although attendance increased somewhat after the Presbyterians began passing out free lunches to the pupils). The missionaries were all quite vocal in condemning traditional Zuni religious beliefs and practices, and they frequently demanded that the U.S. government outlaw traditional Zuni rituals, much to the consternation of the tribe. Zuni religious practices were ultimately not made illegal, but the Zunis began to conduct formerly public ceremonies in private to avoid such censure.

Naturally, American traders accompanied the large flow of people. During the 1870s three white American and two Native American traders established operations at Zuni. At first trade was fairly limited, and traders exchanged manufactured goods for traditional items such as agricultural produce, cloth, jewelry, and pottery. But commerce expanded after 1881 when the Atlantic and Pacific Railroad completed a track to the town of Gallup, New Mexico, located 40 miles northeast of Zuni. Once the railroad was opened, the traders began to purchase sheep and cattle to ship by railroad to national markets in eastern and western states. As a result the Zunis began to raise more herds, which they sold for cash that they used to buy American products.

While the Zuni were increasing their livestock holdings, American sheep-

*Frank Cushing poses in the garb of a Zuni Bow Priest, a rank he attained after his adoption by the tribe in the 1880s. Although Cushing could be aggressive in his dealings with Native American tribes, he remained a vocal advocate of Zuni land and treaty rights throughout his lifetime.*

*Three of the men who accompanied Cushing on a tour of the eastern United States in 1882: (from left) Palowatiwa, a former governor of Zuni; Nanche, a Hopi man adopted into the tribe; and Lai-iu-ah-tsai-ah (also known as Pedro Pino), a former governor of Zuni.*

herders and cattle ranchers entered the Southwest looking for grazing pasture. A steady influx of settlers who encroached on Zuni territory led to increased hostility and competition between the Zunis and the outsiders. As more outsiders arrived, the Zunis demanded that the U.S. government fulfill its obligations under the Treaty of Guadalupe Hidalgo to protect their land. Problems arose immediately because the exact extent of Zuni territory had never been properly surveyed and registered with the U.S. government, and when in 1877 President Rutherford B. Hayes issued an executive order that created the Zuni reservation, the area of land encompassed within the reservation was only about one-tenth the size of territory that Zunis occupied before the European invasions. Many landmarks and areas considered sacred to the Zunis were not included in the reservation boundaries, and many Zunis felt no particular obligation to quit using land they had always regarded as their own because of a proclamation made in some far-off city to the east.

Because of a surveying error, the reservation's borders also did not include several of the Zunis' small farming settlements, among them the village of Nutria and its nearby springs, which were vital to Zuni agriculture. A group of army officers stationed at nearby Fort Wingate had earlier set up a ranch just east of the borders of Zuni territory called the Cibola Cattle Company. When they discovered the surveying error, the officers (who were infamous among the

Zunis for illegally grazing their cattle on reservation lands) attempted to gain title to Nutria and its springs. One of the officers was the son-in-law of a powerful Illinois senator and presidential hopeful named John Logan, who on a tour of the American Southwest had informed the officers of the opportunity to obtain the valuable land. The eastern newspapers were tipped off to the affair by a researcher sent by the Bureau of American Ethnology and an adopted Zuni named Frank Cushing; the result was a tremendous scandal that pitted Logan's vociferous political supporters against his equally vocal opponents. An early casualty of this battle was Cushing, who was finally forced to leave the region by Logan in 1884. (Cushing would later return and continued his entire life to speak out on behalf of the Zunis.)

Fortunately for the Zunis, Senator Logan's landgrab occurred when the tribe actually exercised considerable influence in the East. The Zunis had been the subject of many a flattering popular book and magazine article, beginning with the memoirs of the soldiers feasted by the Zunis during the Mexican War, and had captured the interest and sympathy of many white Americans. In addition, Cushing had arranged a well-publicized tour of the eastern states for several Zuni leaders in 1882. The party had traveled to Chicago, Boston, and Washington D.C., meeting President Chester Arthur and a number of other highly prominent intellectual and business leaders. Many of these influential easterners were favorably impressed by

*A detachment of the Second Calvary camps outside Zuni in 1897. The troops, brought to the village at the request of an American teacher, severely undermined the civil authority of the Bow Priesthood.*

the tribal leaders and became advocates of Zuni land protection; as a result of their efforts, a second executive order was issued in 1883 that added the outlying farm areas, including Nutria and its springs, to the reservation area. A later trip made in 1886 by the Zuni governor and two of his aides helped further publicize the Zunis' cause.

But tours of eastern cities did not prevent both Anglo and Hispanic settlers and ranchers from making more and more inroads into traditional Zuni territories that did not legally form part of the Zuni reservation. Toward the end of the 19th century this encroachment became especially severe on the eastern and southern portions of Zuni land; in the western portion the Mormons were also expanding their holdings. As the

population of immigrant communities grew, the Zuni lost access to most of their former territory, especially areas located near springs and streams, which were especially desirable to settlers. These new settlements prevented the Zunis from grazing their animals, hunting, and gathering wild plants in familiar places that they had used for centuries. Not surprisingly, the result was a number of conflicts over land use, some of them bloody.

American companies also began exploiting the natural resources in Zuni territory during the late 1800s. Timber companies started clear-cutting large portions of forest in the Zuni Mountains in the 1890s. In just over ten years, more than two billion feet of timber were cut— and once the trees were gone, white

American cattle and sheep owners grazed their animals on the deforested land, eliminating any chance of reforestation.

Other Native American groups were also competing for Zuni land. Navajos and Apaches seeking refuge from U.S. Army troops and aggressive white American settlers entered Zuni territory in the mid– and late 19th century and resumed raiding Zuni farms and villages. In one especially serious incident in 1850, more than 100 Navajos held the village of Zuni under siege for 16 days. The Zunis later retaliated by killing 30 Navajos, and Zuni guides and spies assisted U.S. troops in their war against the Navajos (although Zuni traders were an important source of supplies for both Navajo and Apache tribes during their wars with the United States).

The conflicts between the Zunis, Navajos, and Apaches reflected the crowding all of the Native American groups were experiencing as American settlers, backed by U.S. troops, moved onto their lands. Both Navajos and Apaches had been forced out of their traditional territories, and it mattered little to U.S. authorities if the land available for them to live on had historically belonged to another tribe. Eventually the Navajos settled in the northern areas of traditional Zuni territory, while the Apaches settled in the southern and western sections. In 1868 the U.S. government established boundaries for a Navajo reservation that included a northern section of traditional Zuni territory, and three years later, the Apaches

settled on a reservation that took in a southwestern area of traditional Zuni lands. The establishment of such new reservations forced the Zunis to confine themselves more to their relatively small reservation area during a time when their population was finally beginning to increase after centuries of decline.

The Zunis were also faced with increased efforts by missionaries and government officials to interfere with their traditional religious life. In 1897 Mary E. DeSette, the teacher at the Presbyterian day school, had several Bow Priests arrested for persecuting a witch. (She was entirely unaware of and probably equally unconcerned about the complex nature of the crime of witchcraft in Zuni society.) DeSette, who had previously distinguished herself by instigating a haircutting campaign (Zuni men wore long hair) and by threatening to cancel the Shalako festival, was a deeply disruptive force on the reservation, mainly because she felt that the Zunis would respect her and accept her authority only if she, as she put it in a letter to the U.S. Commissioner of Indian Affairs, "stir[red] up the authorities" at every possible occasion. In keeping with this philosophy, DeSette arranged for army troops to aid the local sheriff in arresting the Bow Priests, and although the charges against the priests were dropped and they were released by the government after only a few months (and after having had their hair cut off), at DeSette's request the troops occupied Zuni for nearly a year. According to historian C. Gregory Crampton in his *The*

*Zunis of Cibola*, "throughout the affair the Zunis remained calm, though they may well have had some misgivings about future trends in education." The presence of army troops acting as law enforcement seriously undermined the authority of the Bow Priests; this erosion of authority was intensified because those priests who had had their hair cut off in prison were considered defiled and could no longer participate in important religious ceremonies.

Not surprisingly, the Presbyterian mission did not attract huge numbers of converts at this time, nor did the Christian (Dutch) Reformed Church, which established a mission at Zuni in 1897. As in past centuries, the Zunis' participation in traditional religious societies and rituals oriented their lives around common activities and shared meanings, and giving up such meaningful religious habits did not come easily. In addition, the common demand that Christian converts give up any involvement in traditional Zuni religious practices was completely antithetical to many Zunis, who held that the different religious beliefs were not entirely incompatible. As one missionary lamented, "the most common reaction of Zunis to the gospel message is that the Jesus-way and the Zuni-way are 'hi-ni-na,' 'the same.'"

During the late 19th and early 20th centuries, the U.S. government became more directly involved in regulating the education of Native Americans in general. The federal government had decided that attempts should be made to "civilize" Native Americans by having Native American children attend schools where they could learn American customs and values. English-language instruction was viewed as critical to this effort; consequently, the use of native languages was banned in schools. The U.S. commissioner of Indian affairs clearly enunciated reasons for this policy as far back as 1887, stating,

> Instruction of Indians in the vernacular is not only of no use to them but is detrimental to the cause of education and civilization and will not be permitted in any Indian school. This language which is good enough for a white person ought to be good enough for the red person. It is also believed that teaching Indians in their own barbarous dialect is a positive detriment to them. The impracticability, if not impossibility of civilizing Indians in any other tongue than our own would seem obvious.

After the DeSette affair of 1897, the U.S. government took closer control of the schools at Zuni, ending the subsidizing of mission schools and opening a government day school instead. In addition to the day school, the government opened a boarding school in 1907, and the Christian (Dutch) Reformed Church opened a nonsubsidized mission day school in 1908. These schools offered basic subjects such as writing and reading, cooking and sewing for girls, and manual skills for boys. Such formal education became relatively popular early on, in part because there were now a number of schools on the reservation, so a student who had trouble adjusting at one school could always transfer to a different one. The English-only policy of these schools was initially supported by the Zunis, who felt that their children would learn Zuni at home anyway and that knowledge of English would be a valuable skill when negotiating among Americans. In later years, however, the Zunis would pressure their schools into becoming more bilingual and placing more emphasis on Zuni culture.

The 20th century saw yet another expansion of Zuni agriculture, as Zuni farmers adopted American technology such as plows and iron hoes, shovels, and rakes. Agricultural surpluses were sold for a profit to American traders and residents of nearby towns such as Gallup, New Mexico, and Holbrook, Arizona. The Zuni also sold corn, wheat, and other farm products to soldiers at Fort Defiance and Fort Wingate. Dams and reservoirs were constructed on the Zuni River during the 1900s, creating a more regular supply of water for irrigation. The boom in Zuni farming led to the establishment of a new farming settlement in 1912 called Tekapo (meaning "full of hills"), located southwest of Zuni on the Zuni River.

Zuni ranching also prospered in the early 20th century. By 1910 Zuni ranchers owned about 65,000 head of sheep, more than double the number they had in 1880. The Zuni reservation contained about 285,000 acres, and as the herds grew, the problem of finding

*Girls at the U.S. government–run day school on the Zuni reservation pose for a photograph in 1900. These students were instructed solely in English, a situation that has altered in more recent times as bilingual education has become popular.*

adequate land to graze them on became critical. Zuni leaders and agents of the federal Bureau of Indian Affairs (BIA) repeatedly asked the president and Congress to enlarge the reservation, but instead of adding to Zuni territory, Congress took land away from the reservation in 1910 to create national forests in the area. The Zunis protested, and two years later President William Taft reversed the decision, returning the land. Finally, in 1917, President Woodrow Wilson issued an executive order that added about 80,000 acres to the Zuni reservation. Additional acreage was

*This 1911 photograph shows ground-level doors and windows in Zuni homes. As the need for military defense declined during the 20th century, the use of roof entries reached by ladder became less common.*

included in 1935, bringing the total area up to about 340,000 acres, and in 1940, bringing the total above 400,000 acres. In addition to traditional agricultural sources of income, some Zunis worked for railroads, government agencies, and businesses located in nearby Anglo towns.

Changes also took place in the village of Zuni itself. Although the basic design of Zuni houses did not change, new houses were built with larger rooms and higher ceilings. Defensive concerns were no longer paramount, so ground-level doors and windows became common. In addition, many of the upper-story dwellings were taken down, and more

ground-level homes were built. The Zunis no longer had to cluster all their buildings together for defensive purposes, so outlying houses, built at some distance from the main village, became more common, with 81 families (about 37 percent of the population) living in these "suburbs" by 1915.

The local system of Zuni government also reflected both continuity and change as the 20th century progressed. At the beginning of the century the two governing councils—one consisting of religious leaders whose decisions were enforced by the Bow Priests and one entirely secular in nature, consisting of a governor, a lieutenant governor, and councillors—coexisted and shared power. But the authority of the Bow Priests, already threatened by the DeSette affair, was further undermined when the U.S. government decided to exercise closer control over the Zunis by opening a local BIA office near Zuni in 1902. The new Zuni agency was headed by an agent who supervised federal programs and local activities. BIA agents also advised Zuni secular leaders and had authority to approve or veto decisions of the council.

In 1916 the BIA agent to the Zunis became involved in a controversy that deeply affected Zuni politics. That year a group of Catholic clergy proposed to build a new mission in Zuni. When a public meeting was called to discuss the request, all in attendance signaled their opposition by a voice vote. However, a small group of Zuni Roman Catholics appealed to the BIA agent (himself a Roman Catholic), who donated a plot of village land for the construction of the church. The church, named St. Anthony's Mission Church, was completed in 1922, over the opposition of the majority of the Zunis. Zunis opposed to the mission became known as Protestants (although many were not practitioners of any Christian religion), while those who supported the mission became known as Catholics (whether or not they were actually Roman Catholic)—a political division that has continued to the present day.

In the 1930s a U.S. government study known as the Merriam Report revealed that many Native American tribes lived in abysmally poor conditions. These conditions would be improved, the report suggested, by increased federal funding to the tribes as well as greater tribal control over how such funds were spent. As a result of these findings, Commissioner of Indian Affairs John Collier urged Congress to pass new legislation to give tribal governing councils authority over development programs on their reservations. Although Collier was willing to hand over a considerable amount of power to the tribal councils, he also wanted to regulate their functioning and establish guidelines for selection of councillors in a manner that was not always consistent with tribal traditions.

With Collier's urging, Congress passed legislation known as the Indian Reorganization Act (IRA) in 1934. The IRA provided that the reservations adopt formal constitutions and elect their tribal leaders. Each reservation had the option of accepting or rejecting the IRA's provisions through a local referendum. Andrew Trotter, the BIA superintendent in charge of the Zuni Agency, was instrumental in convincing the Zunis (who at the time were in the midst of a bitter dispute between the Catholics and the Protestants that threatened to render the village ungovernable) to adopt the IRA provisions. Once the IRA was accepted, Trotter appointed a nominating committee of six members to nominate two candidates for the position of governor. After the nominations were made, a public meeting was held at which all men in attendance could vote. The candidate who received the

*St. Anthony's Mission Church, rebuilt in 1922. The rebuilding of a Roman Catholic church in Zuni caused intense conflict and division among the tribe.*

most votes became governor, while the losing candidate became lieutenant governor. In addition to the gubernatorial election, six members of a tribal council were also selected, each representing a different district. Under the new regulations, all tribal leaders served for terms of one year. The nominating committee appointed by Trotter functioned for two years, after which members of the committee were elected by male voters until 1965, when women obtained the franchise. Obviously, this new system of choosing leaders was extremely different from the traditional system, wherein religious leaders appointed the members of the local government. According to Crampton, "The transition from a theocratic form of government to one based on popular consent was not achieved without much division and debate, anxiety, stress, tension, and soul-searching. People still take sides on the form of government the Zunis should have."

The 1930s witnessed other federal initiatives that also had long-term consequences for the Zunis. For the first time since the reservation was established in 1877, the government carried out an extensive survey of the boundaries of Zuni land. When the survey was completed in 1934, government workers erected a fence around the reservation's borders. Prior to this time, Zuni herders had routinely grazed their animals in adjacent pastures, but after the reservation was fenced in, they were restricted to the land within the reservation. This reduction in grazing area quickly resulted in a depletion of good forage and erosion of the soil. In response to the worsening situation, Collier instituted a program of stock reduction aimed at limiting the number of animals owned by Native Americans. The Zuni reservation was divided into 18 grazing units, and each was given a quota of livestock based on what federal authorities thought the unit could sustain. If herders in the unit had holdings that exceeded the limit, they were forced to sell the surplus animals to the government at fixed prices.

The Zunis vigorously protested the stock-reduction program. Zuni herders had never been consulted during the development of this program, and they resented what they saw as a high-handed interference with their livelihood. Many families had to give up a large portion of their herds, thereby losing a stable source of income. The prices paid herders for their sheep by the government were low, and a one-time payment for herds did not reflect the sheep's true value, since herders sold wool from the same animals year after year. Despite these losses, Zuni herders made a slow economic recovery after World War II.

The 1940s also saw over 200 Zuni men leave the village to fight for the United States in World War II. Many of them were exposed to new countries and new cultures, and some of them came back expounding ideas and exhibiting behavior their elders found distinctly non-Zuni, which resulted for a short while in a good deal of generational friction. The veterans quickly reintegrated themselves into Zuni life, however, participating in dances and religious ceremonies and utilizing their G.I. benefits to obtain vocational and agricultural training. By midcentury the Zunis had adjusted to changed conditions brought about by pressures from outside forces, incorporating new technologies and activities into their lives while keeping faith in their own values and beliefs. ▲

*A Zuni silversmith creates her wares. Silversmithing and other forms of craft production have become important sources of income for Zunis in the 20th century.*

# THE
# ZUNI
# TODAY

The Zuni reservation currently consists of 409,134 acres, or 636 square miles of land and, according to the 1990 census, is home to 7,073 people (3,625 women and 3,448 men)—a dramatic recovery in this century from the low of 1,514 people recorded in 1905. Census data also indicates the continued strength of Zuni families: 97 percent of the Zunis reside in family-based households, while only 3 percent live alone or with non-family members. The percentage of Zuni households based on family membership is the highest among all U.S. population groups.

Many changes have taken place in the Zunis' lives. The reservation itself has undergone modernization in terms of housing, public services, and transportation. In the 1950s improvements were made in public services that included the installation of electricity, the construction of a piped water system, the paving of roads, and the completion of a sewer system and indoor plumbing. The community of Zuni now contains two distinct types of housing.

In the old central section of town, the houses primarily retain the traditional Zuni designs, although they have been modernized and enlarged. New homes—mostly single-family dwellings, some with small lawns—have been constructed in suburban areas outside Zuni. These homes are of various styles, some with gabled or pitched roofs and some built from wood, cinder block, and other materials. The community at Blackrock, the site of the BIA agency, located several miles to the northeast of Zuni, has also increased. An airstrip was built there in 1967, and the community is also now the home of a hospital run by the public health service. The location of traditional kivas and open plazas has remained the same, but new public facilities have been added to Zuni, including a large building that contains the headquarters of the tribal council and other government offices. Five schools now serve the reservation.

The Zuni economy has grown and diversified since the middle of the 20th century. Sources of income include farming, herding, wage work, and craft production. Farming continues to be an important endeavor, although most rely on farming only for supplemental income. Only about 1,000 acres of Zuni land are currently under cultivation, a sharp decrease from the 10,000–12,000 acres farmed a century ago. Major crops today include corn, pinto beans, wheat, chili, cabbage, onions, and beets, which are either consumed in the household or sold to nearby markets. As in past centuries, most farming is done by men, although a number of older women still plant small traditional waffle gardens near their homes.

The Zunis have expanded and upgraded water supplies to increase farm production and livestock holdings, digging numerous wells throughout the reservation to provide water for livestock and developing the natural springs at Nutria, Pescado, and Ojo Caliente. Approximately 95 percent of the reservation's land is now used for grazing. The reservation is divided into 95 grazing units for sheepherding, each assigned to a specific herder or group of herders. Four pastures for cattle are assigned to two cattle associations. As of 1992 the Zunis owned some 10,735 sheep, 122 goats, 1,767 cattle, and 32 horses.

All use of grazing land is regulated by provisions of the Zuni Range Code, adopted in 1976. The code issues permits to herders and sets limits for the number of animals allowed in each grazing unit or cattle range. If owners exceed their annual quotas, they must sell the sur-

plus. The Zuni A:shiwi Livestock Committee was formed in 1992 to supervise use of rangelands. It updates and enforces the range code, recommends range improvements, and resolves any conflicts that arise over use of land. Improvements have been made in rangelands through tribal programs that reseed the land, remove unwanted trees, and restore pasture.

The Zunis are developing additional uses of their land in order to provide tribal and individual income. Deposits of sand, gravel, and limestone are mined by public and private concerns for the construction and paving of roads on and near the reservation. At one time the BIA operated four mines to exploit the substantial coal deposits near Nutria and Pescado. These mines are now defunct but may be reopened in the future, as may the historic copper mines in the Zuni Mountains. The Zunis have also stocked their reservoirs with fish for recreational purposes.

Most Zuni families support themselves through wage work. Even among families who are engaged in farming or herding, some members usually have jobs and contribute their salaries to the household. Some people work in the public sector, in office or maintenance positions for tribal and federal agencies. Others seek employment in local businesses and industries or tribal enterprises. And some work in nearby towns (especially Gallup) as construction workers, nurses, and employees of restaurants and stores. Despite the range of jobs, rates of unemployment and under-

*Traditional outdoor ovens sit in front of a modern dwelling. Although most homes now have electricity, many Zunis prefer to cook traditional dishes such as cornbread in the customary manner.*

*One of the tribe's six kivas, located in the old section of Zuni.*

employment are high among the Zunis because the actual number of jobs in the area is fairly low.

Many Zunis are self-employed as silversmiths or artisans. Silver work, which began as an occupation for men, is now practiced by women as well, and in many cases, husbands and wives form a team, allocating separate tasks in the process of jewelry-making to each spouse. Zuni silversmiths produce jewelry in two distinctive styles, needlepoint and inlay. In the needlepoint style, small bits of turquoise are cut and mounted in silver to form patterns on rings, necklaces, bracelets, and pins. In the inlay technique, small pieces of shell, coral, jet, and turquoise are cut into different shapes and then mounted in a base of silver. Silversmiths sell their jewelry to traders in Gallup, Santa Fe, Albuquerque, and many other cities. Two organizations, the Zuni Craftsmen's Cooperative Association and the Zuni Arts and Crafts Enterprise, market jewelry to both local and national outlets and promote silversmiths, potters, painters, and sculptors.

Some Zuni artists produce objects called fetishes that have great religious significance. Fetishes are representative images of deities made of wood and decorated with paint and feathers. Zuni artists have been making sacred fetishes for centuries, but many of the older fetishes were bought or stolen from the tribe by visitors and were eventually acquired by museums and private galleries and collectors. In 1978 the Zunis began to seek the return of their sacred objects, and by 1992, 63 such objects had been returned by museums such as the Smithsonian Institution in Washington, D.C., the Museum of the American Indian in New York City, and the Museum of New Mexico in Albuquerque. Private galleries and individual collectors have also returned several fetishes. Another result of the Zunis' efforts to repossess their fetishes was the passage in Congress of the Native American Grave Protection and Rehabilitation Act of 1990, which provides for the return of Native American artifacts and grave remains to the tribe from which they were taken.

The political structure of the tribe underwent a good deal of change during the 1970s. In 1970 the Zunis adopted a formal constitution, and the U.S. government recognized the Zuni Tribal Council as the Zunis' official legislative and executive body, with the right to control the local government and organize elections. In 1974 the Zunis eliminated the nominating committee and instituted popular elections in which candidates run on their own behalf. The governor, lieutenant governor, and members of the tribal council are now elected to four-year terms. The current governor, Robert Lewis, was first elected to office in 1965 and has served most of the terms since then.

One area of critical concern for the tribal council, and for all Zunis, is land rights and compensation for land taken illegally during the past centuries. The Zunis lobbied for the return of Zuni Salt Lake, which not only provides salt but is an important religious site. In 1978 the

*Many Zunis now support themselves through wage work. This Zuni man is showing two tourists some of the historical landmarks of the reservation.*

U.S. Congress enacted legislation directing the federal government to acquire Zuni Salt Lake from the state of New Mexico and to return it to the tribe. The Zunis now possess a lease to the lake.

A dispute over another sacred area recently ended in victory for the Zunis. The tribe filed a suit for the return of a site called Koluwala-wa, located at the juncture of the Zuni and Little Colorado rivers. Koluwala-wa is the focus of pilgrimages made every four years by religious leaders who ask deities there for rain to nurture the land and crops, and it is one of the places where Zuni souls

go after death. In 1984 the Zunis won the return of Koluwala-wa, but they were sometimes denied access to the area by ranchers who owned surrounding land. After years of protest in court, the Zunis were granted the permanent right to cross private land on their ritual journeys to Koluwala-wa.

In addition to suits for the return of land, the Zunis submitted a claim to the U.S. Court of Claims in 1978 for monetary compensation for land taken from them in the 19th and 20th centuries. The Court of Claims issued a ruling in 1987 giving the Zunis title to a large portion of present-day Arizona and New Mexico and stating that the tribe had been wrongfully deprived of 14,835,892 acres of their land during the period from 1876 to 1939. Following years of negotiation, the Zunis were awarded $25 million as compensation for their land. The award was deposited in a trust fund and is awaiting the tribe's decision on how to put it to best use.

In 1990 the Zunis reached an agreement with the U.S. government that ended another legal suit. In the 1970s the Zunis had sued the government for neglecting its responsibilities to protect Zuni land, as pledged in the treaties signed between the two nations. The tribe claimed that the U.S. government had illegally sold Zuni land to a number of non-Zunis, including railroad companies that were extending track through the Southwest at the turn of the 20th century and officers stationed at Fort Wingate who wished to open private ranches. In addition, the U.S. government permitted ranchers to encroach on and to overgraze Zuni land, and it allowed timber companies to overcut Zuni forests. Finally, the U.S. government permitted the mining of coal and salt from Zuni territory without compensating the tribe.

The Zunis' suit against the United States ended in an agreement ratified by Congress as the Zuni Land Conservation Act of 1990, which established a permanent Zuni Indian Resource Development Trust Fund, consisting of $17 million. Interest from the fund is used to create and implement the Zuni Sus-

*An archaeological dig exhumes Zuni remains in this photograph, taken during the 1890s. The tribe actively lobbied for the passage of the Native American Grave Protection and Rehabilitation Act of 1990, which provides for the return of pilfered remains and grave artifacts.*

*A group of Zuni girls pose in front of St. Anthony's High School before performing in a school play. Despite centuries of foreign rule, the Zunis have successfully preserved both their culture and their people.*

tainable Resource Development Plan, aimed at developing renewable resources on the reservation, rehabilitating the reservation's watershed and water resources, and acquiring land for future use. The Zuni Sustainable Resource Development Plan is overseen and implemented by the Zuni Conservation Project, directed by James Enote, which aims to replant vegetation, control soil erosion, improve soil quality, and reduce the loss of water. The Conservation Project collects data on fish and wildlife resources, water sources, and forestry needs, and it began a pilot program at Nutria in 1992 to gather data on local conditions, including the quality of soil, water resources, crop needs, and labor skills of Zuni farmers.

Another land conservation program is the Zuni Sustainable Agriculture Project, dedicated to developing local agriculture. Project workers study soil management issues such as irrigation procedures and soil quality. They are currently investigating the possibility of reestablishing peach orchards originally planted during the period of Spanish conquest on the mesa at Dowa Yallane and expanding production of alfalfa.

Other tribal projects seek to preserve the Zunis' cultural heritage and advance the tribe's opportunities for the future. The A:shiwi A:wan Museum and Heritage Center (*A:shiwi A:wan* means "belonging to the Zuni people") was founded as a center for maintaining, dis-

playing, and enhancing knowledge of Zuni history and culture. In the words of the museum's statement of purpose, it is not a "temple" for the past, but "a community learning center which links the past with the present as a strategy to deal with the future." The museum has a tribal archive that keeps documents of all tribal activities, and it publishes a quarterly newsletter containing information about programs at the museum and elsewhere in the community. News about local events and current issues is also relayed on the Zunis' own radio station, KSHI-FM, founded in 1977.

The Zunis proudly maintain many aspects of their traditional culture. Families are bound together with strong feelings of communal loyalty and support, and matrilineal clans continue to determine an individual's social and group identity. The Zuni language is still the first language of most people. And the entire community unites to celebrate sacred rituals that have as much meaning for modern Zunis as they did for their ancestors. In the words of a Zuni storyteller,

Today as we live in the present ways of our people, we live also within the realm of our ancestors, for we are sustained through the rituals and beliefs of long ago. We live in accordance to the ways of our people, which bring life, blessings, and happiness. ▲

# BIBLIOGRAPHY

Crampton, C. Gregory. *The Zunis of Cibola*. Salt Lake City: University of Utah Press, 1977.

Cushing, Frank Hamilton. *Cushing at Zuni: The Correspondence and Journals of Frank Hamilton Cushing 1879–1884*. Edited by Jesse Green. Albuquerque: University of New Mexico Press, 1990.

———. *Zuñi Folk Tales*. 1901. Reprint. Tucson: University of Arizona Press, 1986.

———. *Zuñi: Selected Writings of Frank Hamilton Cushing*. Edited by Jesse Green. Lincoln: University of Nebraska Press, 1979.

Morris, John Miller. *From Coronado to Escalante: The Explorers of the Spanish Southwest*. New York: Chelsea House, 1992.

Ortiz, Alfonso, ed. *Handbook of North American Indians. Southwest*. Vol. 9. Washington, D.C.: Smithsonian Institution, 1979.

———. *The Pueblo*. New York: Chelsea House, 1994.

Tedlock, Barbara. *The Beautiful and the Dangerous: Encounters with the Zuni Indians*. New York: Viking, 1992.

Wilson, Edmund. *Red, Black, Blond and Olive: Studies in Four Civilizations: Zuñi, Haiti, Soviet Russia, Israel*. New York: Oxford University Press, 1956.

Wright, Barton. *Kachinas of the Zuni*. Flagstaff, AZ: Northland Press, 1985.

The Zuni People. *Zunis: Self-Portrayals*. Translated by Alvian Quam. Albuquerque: University of New Mexico Press, 1972.

# THE ZUNI AT A GLANCE

TRIBE  *Zuni*
CULTURE AREA  *Southwest*
GEOGRAPHY  *New Mexico*
LINGUISTIC FAMILY  *Possibly Penutian*
CURRENT POPULATION  *Approximately 7,070*
FEDERAL STATUS  *Tribal reservation in New Mexico*

*agent* A person appointed by the Bureau of Indian Affairs to supervise U.S. government programs on a reservation and/or in a specific region.

*Awonawilona* The deity, who is both male and female, responsible for creating the universe.

*Bow Priesthood* A prestigious group whose members were responsible for carrying out warfare and keeping order in the villages.

*Bureau of Indian Affairs (BIA)* A federal government agency, now within the Department of the Interior, founded to manage relations with Native American tribes.

*clan* A multigenerational group having a shared identity, organization, and property based on belief in their descent from a common ancestor. Because clan members consider themselves closely related, marriage within a clan is strictly prohibited.

*culture* The learned behavior of humans; nonbiological, socially taught activities; the way of life of a group of people.

*ethnologist* An anthropologist who specializes in comparing and analyzing different cultures.

*fetish* A representative image of a deity made of wood and decorated with paint and feathers. Besides being a work of art, a fetish has great religious significance.

*Indian Reorganization Act (IRA)* The 1934 federal law that ended the policy of allotting plots of land to individuals and encouraged the development of reservation communities. The act also provided for the creation of autonomous tribal governments.

*itiwana* The middle place of the world, where the Zunis were told to settle after emerging from the inside of the earth in their creation legend.

*kachinas* Souls of the dead who are impersonated by Zunis wearing special costumes and performing elaborate public dances. All Zuni men were members of one of the six kachina societies.

*kiva* A special square-shaped room, entered by a ladder through the ceiling, where religious ceremonies are held.

*Koyemshi* An ancient group of Raw People who are impersonated throughout the year. Also called the Mudheads, each Koyemshi acts like a clown but is considered to have great power to bring good fortune and rain.

*lhamana* A Zuni man who wore the clothing and performed the work traditionally associated with women. Lhamana (also known as berdaches) were considered by tribal members to be of a third gender, distinct from both males and females.

*matrilineal* A kinship system based on descent from the woman's lineage.

*Merriam Report* A U.S. government study in the 1930s that found appalling conditions of poverty on many reservations and suggested increased federal funding to Native American tribes.

*metate* A specialized grinding stone for making meal out of seeds, nuts, and corn.

*Native American Grave Protection and Rehabilitation Act of 1990* A Congressional resolution that allows Native American tribes to repossess the artifacts and grave remains that were taken from them by museums and individual collectors.

*Neweekwe* Members of a Zuni medicine society who specialize in curing stomach ailments, the Neweekwe engage in sophisticated forms of clowning.

*pekwin* The head of Zuni village government who was appointed by the council of priests and worked with them to manage collective work, community affairs, and religious ceremonies. The pekwin was required to be a member of the Dogwood clan as well as a kind and respected individual.

*Rain Priesthood* The most powerful priesthood, whose members derived their knowledge and powers from the Rain-Bringing Spirits and who performed rituals that would bring rain to the Zunis.

*Raw People* The many powerful deities and spirits in the Zuni religion, named for the raw food given to them as offerings from humans. The Zuni also say prayers and perform rituals in the Raw People's honor, and in exchange the Raw People provide protection and good fortune.

*reservation* A tract of land retained by Indians for their own occupation and use.

*Shalakos* Six powerful, birdlike beings who are impersonated by select Zuni men every fall and bring abundant crops and many children.

*Treaty of Guadalupe Hidalgo* The treaty that ended the Mexican War in 1848 and granted the United States ownership of present-day Arizona and New Mexico. In the treaty, the U.S. government promised to respect the land and rights of the native peoples in the region.

*tribe* A society consisting of several separate communities united by kinship, culture, language, and other social institutions, including clans, religious organizations, and warrior societies.

*Zuni Land Conservation Act of 1990* As settlement of a Zuni lawsuit against the government, Congress established the permanent Zuni Indian Resource Development Trust Fund of $17 million. Interest from the fund supports the Zuni Sustainable Resource Development Plan.

*Zuni Tribal Council* Recognized by the U.S. government in the early 1970s, the Zunis' official legislative and executive body has the right to control the local government and organize elections.

# INDEX

# PICTURE CREDITS

NANCY BONVILLAIN is an adjunct professor at the New School for Social Research. She has a Ph.D. in anthropology from Columbia University. Dr. Bonvillain has written a grammar book and dictionary of the Mohawk language as well as *The Huron* (1989), *The Mohawk* (1992), and *Black Hawk* (1994) for Chelsea House.

---

FRANK W. PORTER III, general editor of INDIANS OF NORTH AMERICA, is director of the Chelsea House Foundation for American Indian Studies. He holds a B.A., M.A., and Ph.D. from the University of Maryland. He has done extensive research concerning the Indians of Maryland and Delaware and is the author of numerous articles on their history, archaeology, geography, and ethnography. He was formerly director of the Maryland Commission on Indian Affairs and American Indian Research and Resource Institute, Gettysburg, Pennsylvania, and he has received grants from the Delaware Humanities Forum, the Maryland Committee for the Humanities, the Ford Foundation, and the National Endowment for the Humanities, among others. Dr. Porter is the author of *The Bureau of Indian Affairs* in the Chelsea House KNOW YOUR GOVERNMENT series.